The MAILBOX

The Education Center

M000110535

Math Practice Pages

Over **80** engaging reproducibles for building **number and operations skills!**

- Number Sense
- Addition & Subtraction
- Multiplication

- Division
- Fractions
- Decimals

Use to reteach, reinforce, and assess!

Managing Editor: Amy Payne

Editorial Team: Becky S. Andrews, Diane Badden, Kimberley Bruck, Karen A. Brudnak, Kitty Campbell, Chris Curry, Lynette Dickerson, Theresa Lewis Goode, Tazmen Hansen, Marsha Heim, Lori Z. Henry, Debra Liverman, Dorothy C. McKinney, Thad H. McLaurin, Sharon Murphy, Jennifer Nunn, Mark Rainey, Hope Rodgers, Eliseo De Jesus Santos II, Becky Saunders, Barry Slate, Zane Williard

www.themailbox.com

©2008 The Mailbox® Books
All rights reserved.
ISBN10 #1-56234-796-9 • ISBN13 #978-156234-796-3

Manufactured in the United States
10 9 8 7 6 5 4 3 2 1

Table of Contents

Fractions

Decimals

Scoot Along

Write each number in standard form.

A. four hundred fifty-one thousand, four hundred twenty-three _____

B. five million, seven hundred eighty-two thousand,
   nine hundred forty-one
   _____

C. four hundred twenty-eight _____

D. four thousand, five hundred eighty-six _____

E. fifty-four thousand, six hundred thirty-nine _____

F. eighty-four thousand, two hundred thirty-five _____

Write each number in word form.

G. 5,649 _____

_____

H. 6,791,256 _____

_____

I. 843,214 _____

_____

J. 7,879 _____

_____

Funny Food

Circle the digit in the place value named.
Then write each letter on its matching numbered line or lines to solve each riddle.

Why did the doughnut go to the dentist?

___ ___   ___ ___ ___   ___   ___ ___ ___ ___ ___ ___
3   1   5   8   3   4   2   6   9   9   6   7   5

E. tens
34,589

A. hundreds
679,486

F. thousands
3,402,257

T. millions
3,456,780

G. ones
49,375

O. tens
901,213

I. hundred thousands
604,634

L. millions
9,823,659

N. ten thousands
872,312

What is a termite's favorite breakfast?

" ___ ___ ___ - ___ ___ ___ ___ "
  1   4   6   7   2   5   3

O. thousands
21,323

L. tens
405,334

A. ones
5,124

E. ten thousands
225,346

M. hundreds
33,755

A. millions
5,234,365

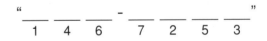

K. hundred thousands
5,664,345

Run for the Roses

Round each number to the underlined place value.
Cross out the matching answer. Not all numbers will be used.

A. 5̲8
60

B. 3,2̲53,287

C. 9̲32

D. 4,̲164,892

E. 4̲4

F. 1̲22

G. 5̲6,626

H. 7̲,299

I. 2̲50,773

J. 9̲8,620

K. 33,9̲68

L. 22̲1

M. 1̲1

N. 2,4̲50

O. 6̲14

3,300,000   40
300,000   ~~60~~   20
50   1,000
4,000,000   56,000   3,200,000
57,000   200
7,000   220   34,000
2,500   250,000   100
100,000   5,000,000
600   900   8,000
50
10

Math Practice Pages • ©The Mailbox® Books • TEC61122 • Key p. 87

Rounding to millions

Name _____   Date _____

Asteroid Belt

Compare. Use >, <, or =.
Color the matching symbol.

A. 1,423 〇 1,243

B. 632 〇 633

C. 20,515 〇 20,155

D. 419 〇 491

E. 3,646,177 〇 3,664,177

F. 3,422 〇 3,422

G. 3,986 〇 3,968

H. 481,540 〇 418,504

I. 75,611 〇 76,411

J. 52,432 〇 52,342

K. 725 〇 572

L. 93,111 〇 93,111

M. 234,842 〇 324,842

N. 794,237 〇 749,327

O. 532 〇 532

Name _____ Date _____

Splish, Splash

Add.

A.   89
    + 74

B.   77
    + 64

C.   65
    + 57

D.   87
    + 54

E.   79
    + 73

F.   89
    + 67

G.   59
    + 53

H.   95
    + 65

I.   94
    + 59

J.   89
    + 26

K.   83
    + 48

L.   76
    + 47

M.   98
    + 23

N.   89
    + 72

O.   94
    + 86

P.   86
    + 85

Q.   86
    + 37

R.   68
    + 62

S.   65
    + 47

T.   79
    + 67

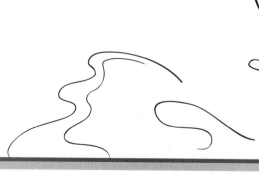

U.   77
    + 73

V.   95
    + 49

W.   74
    + 58

X.   87
    + 53

Addition with regrouping

Waiting for the Bus

Add. Cross out each answer below.

A.   459
   + 48

B.   576
   + 87

C.   3,481
   + 219

D.   4,393
   + 859

E.   787
   + 54

F.   4,727
   + 963

G.   235
   + 86

H.   698
   + 68

I.   7,502
   + 735

J.   749
   + 75

K.   5,456
   + 251

L.   554
   + 68

M.   689
   + 41

N.   2,076
   + 583

O.   315
   + 98

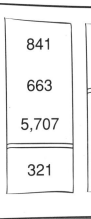

841	622	766	730
663		3,700	
5,707	2,659	8,237	824
			5,690
321	5,252	413	507

STOP

Name _____

Date _____

Going for a Swim

Subtract. Color each fish with a matching answer.

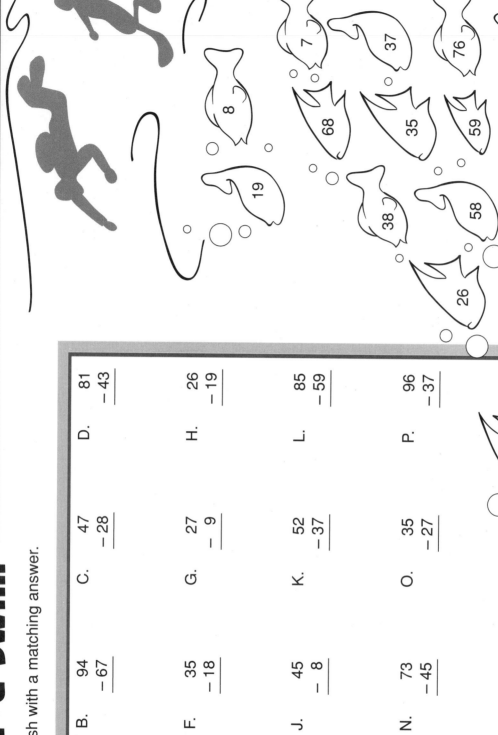

A.	82 − 6	B.	94 −67	C.	47 −28	D.	81 −43
E.	73 −38	F.	35 −18	G.	27 − 9	H.	26 −19
I.	24 −18	J.	45 − 8	K.	52 −37	L.	85 −59
M.	75 − 7	N.	73 −45	O.	35 −27	P.	96 −37
Q.	63 − 5	R.	61 −25				

Subtraction with regrouping

Meet in the Middle

Subtract. Circle each odd answer to reveal the path.

```
  6,617          1,564              665
 -  234         -  377             - 548
```

```
                                   963
                                 -  483
   462           720
 -   77         - 518              760
                                 -  14
```

```
                 554              175
               - 238             -  82
  3,538
 -  624
```

```
   456          1,656
 -  169         -  429
   320          7,287
 -  286         -  824
```

Give and Take

Solve.

A.
```
    31
  −  4
```

B.
```
    58
  + 29
```

C.
```
    42
  − 37
```

D.
```
   275
  −  93
```

E.
```
    48
  + 68
```

F.
```
   467
  +  87
```

G.
```
  7,818
  +  786
```

H.
```
   859
  − 476
```

I.
```
    54
  −  9
```

J.
```
   610
  −  28
```

K.
```
  8,622
  −   323
```

L.
```
  6,794
  + 3,059
```

M.
```
    86
  −  8
```

N.
```
   326
  +  74
```

O.
```
    77
  + 48
```

P.
```
  3,689
  +  847
```

Q.
```
  5,824
  −   569
```

R.
```
  3,185
  + 1,182
```

S.
```
   168
  +  63
```

T.
```
   793
  − 625
```

Math Practice Pages • ©The Mailbox® Books • TEC61122 • Key p. 88

Adding and subtracting with regrouping

DJ Favorites

Subtract. Circle the letter of each even answer.

A. 407 − 253	H. 4,700 − 186	E. 900 − 618	G. 3,903 − 692	A. 8,500 − 816

D. 700 − 694	B. 4,070 − 794	I. 704 − 325	A. 5,041 − 785

N. 2,007 − 575	H. 600 − 475	M. 7,106 − 625	J. 760 − 531

F. 3,000 − 983	L. 530 − 273	D. 6,010 − 478

K. 170 − 121	C. 1,906 − 237

What makes music on your head?

To solve the riddle, write each circled letter from above in order from left to right, top to bottom, on the lines below.

___ ___ ___ ___ ___ ___ ___ ___ ___ !

Name _____ Date _____

Ice Cream for Sale

Solve.

Homemade
Ice Cream

A. Pedro sold 156 double-dip ice cream cones. Carrie sold 75 double-dip cones. How many double-dip ice cream cones did they sell in all?

B. Pedro sold 359 ice cream sandwiches last month. He sold 57 ice cream sandwiches this month. How many ice cream sandwiches did he sell in all?

C. In the morning, Pedro made 435 chocolate shakes. In the afternoon he made 68. How many more shakes did he make in the morning?

F. Carrie sold 3,486 ice cream cones in one month. Pedro sold 6,430 ice cream cones in the same month. How many ice cream cones were sold altogether?

D. On Sunday, 4,672 people bought ice cream. On Monday, 539 bought ice cream. How many people bought ice cream altogether?

G. Pedro made 817 ice cream sundaes. Carrie made 639 banana splits. How many more ice cream sundaes were made than banana splits?

E. There were 925 people who asked for chocolate ice cream. Then 468 people asked for strawberry ice cream. How many fewer people asked for strawberry than chocolate ice cream?

H. On Thursday, 396 gallons of milk were used. On Friday, 709 gallons of milk were used. How many more gallons were used on Friday than Thursday?

Name _____ Date _____

In the Jungle

Round each number to its greatest place value. Then estimate each sum or difference.

A. 54
   + 93
   ‾‾‾‾

B. 350
   + 240
   ‾‾‾‾

C. 860
   − 540
   ‾‾‾‾

D. 53
   − 48
   ‾‾‾‾

E. 25
   + 44
   ‾‾‾‾

F. 500
   + 190
   ‾‾‾‾

G. 530
   − 310
   ‾‾‾‾

H. 42
   − 34
   ‾‾‾‾

I. 470
   − 210
   ‾‾‾‾

J. 280
   + 760
   ‾‾‾‾

K. 520
   − 480
   ‾‾‾‾

L. 720
   + 940
   ‾‾‾‾

M. 86
   + 22
   ‾‾‾‾

N. 410
   − 390
   ‾‾‾‾

O. 610
   + 650
   ‾‾‾‾

Treasure Hunt

Multiply. Color the space of each correct answer to reveal the path.

3 x 5 = 15

8 x 3 = 24

9 x 4 = 36

9 x 5 = 45

3 x 3 = 6

6 x 2 = 12

5 x 5 = 25

3 x 4 = 12

5 x 1 = 5

5 x 4 = 24

4 x 4 = 8

8 x 2 = 14

7 x 4 = 24

6 x 1 = 7

8 x 5 = 40

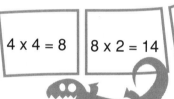

3 x 6 = 15

5 x 7 = 35

6 x 4 = 24

7 x 1 = 8

7 x 3 = 21

9 x 2 = 18

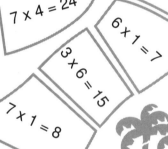

4 x 2 = 6

5 x 6 = 30

8 x 4 = 32

Name _____   Date _____

"Bee" Careful!

Multiply. Color the bees with the matching answers.

A. 7
   x 7

B. 8
   x 9

C. 7
   x 8

D. 3
   x 9

E. 8
   x 8

F. 2
   x 7

G. 7
   x 6

H. 10
   x 8

I. 5
   x 8

J. 12
   x 2

K. 3
   x 7

L. 9
   x 9

M. 11
   x 7

N. 6
   x 6

O. 11
   x 5

P. 9
   x 6

Q. 8
   x 6

R. 10
   x 9

S. 7
   x 9

T. 12
   x 5

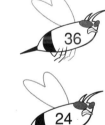

Three Times a Day

Round to the greatest place value to estimate each product.

A.   26
  x 3

B.   624
  x 2

C.   458
  x 3

D.   56
  x 2

E.   94
  x 9

F.   672
  x 2

G.   206
  x 2

H.   67
  x 4

I.   367
  x 3

J.   129
  x 6

K.   76
  x 8

L.   533
  x 3

M.   82
  x 7

N.   410
  x 2

O.   59
  x 9

Skydiving Duo

Round to the greatest place value to estimate each product.

A. 25 x 53 =

B. 91 x 36 =

C. 50 x 72 =

D. 17 x 42 =

E. 72 x 86 =

F. 38 x 95 =

G. 42 x 76 =

H. 36 x 71 =

I. 56 x 47 =

J. 87 x 22 =

K. 32 x 26 =

L. 54 x 12 =

M. 96 x 60 =

N. 89 x 31 =

O. 97 x 41 =

Go Team

Solve.

1. The cheerleading squad practices each day for 95 minutes. They practice five days a week. About how many minutes do they practice each week?

2. There are 17 members on the cheerleading squad. Each member made three posters to support the football team. About how many posters did the squad make?

3. The halftime show at each game lasts 298 seconds. The squad performs at seven games. About how many seconds do they perform?

4. One uniform costs $98. There are 17 cheerleaders on the squad. About how much money does it cost to buy uniforms for all the cheerleaders?

5. The squad held a bake sale. Eight members of the squad each made 144 cookies. About how many cookies were made?

6. Fifteen cheerleaders agreed to clean the field after the last football game. They each filled 17 trash bags. About how many bags of trash were filled?

Name _____   Date _____

Cooling Off

Multiply.
Cross out each matching answer.

A. 31 × 23	B. 13 × 13	C. 17 × 11	D. 42 × 20	E. 21 × 14	F. 37 × 11

G. 14 × 12	H. 41 × 12	I. 33 × 13	J. 32 × 21	K. 40 × 22	L. 34 × 21

M. 29 × 11	N. 22 × 14	O. 53 × 11

In the Dark

Multiply.
Lightly color the correct answers to reveal the path.

Start

18 x 10 180	44 x 22 968
37 x 11 517	34 x 22 746	23 x 12 276

32 x 31 992	75 x 11 825	42 x 21 881	33 x 23 759	19 x 11 209	43 x 20 860
51 x 11 561	32 x 13 415	24 x 21 504	43 x 12 516		
40 x 20 800	16 x 10 170	62 x 10 730			
70 x 10 700	44 x 12 528				

Finish

Girls' Cabin

Boys' Cabin

Name _____   Date _____

Ring-a-Duck

Multiply.

A. 23
   x 23

B. 34
   x 20

C. 31
   x 13

E. 44
   x 21

F. 24
   x 12

K. 17
   x 10

O. 87
   x 11

Q. 33
   x 22

R. 13
   x 11

S. 41
   x 21

U. 19
   x 11

X. 22
   x 14

Ring-
a-Duck

What do you call a box filled with ducks?
To solve the riddle, write each letter from above
on its matching numbered line or lines below.

___ ___ ___ ___ ___ ___   ___ ___ ___ ___ ___ ___ ___ ___ !
529   680 957 308   957 288   726 209 529 403 170 924 143 861

Name _____   Date _____

"Moo-sic"

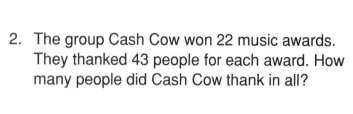

Solve.

1. Moo-Z has made 14 music videos. Each video has 21 backup singers. How many backup singers are there in all?

2. The group Cash Cow won 22 music awards. They thanked 43 people for each award. How many people did Cash Cow thank in all?

3. Mooria wrote 12 songs. She spent 31 minutes writing each song. How many minutes did she spend in all?

4. Cowtown Records has signed 11 new singers. Each singer will perform a concert 35 times this year. How many concerts will be performed in all?

5. There are 44 music store owners who want Moo-Z to sign autographs at their stores. Moo-Z will sign 20 autographs at each store. How many autographs will Moo-Z sign in all?

6. Cowtown Records ordered 13 boxes of T-shirts to give away. Each box has 23 shirts. How many T-shirts did Cowtown order to give away?

Name _____   Date _____

If the Shoe Fits

Multiply.
Color the shoe with the matching answer. Not all shoes will be colored.

A. 17
    x 14

B. 16
    x 12

C. 15
    x 31

D. 12
    x 80

E. 16
    x 51

F. 36
    x 13

G. 17
    x 12

H. 18
    x 12

I. 16
    x 15

J. 17
    x 13

K. 26
    x 14

L. 47
    x 12

M. 37
    x 12

N. 16
    x 14

O. 25
    x 13

 216
 220
 364
 468
 325
 221
 240
 444
 564
 816
 209

238   224   465   449   192   204   960

Rich Dreams

Multiply. Color if correct.

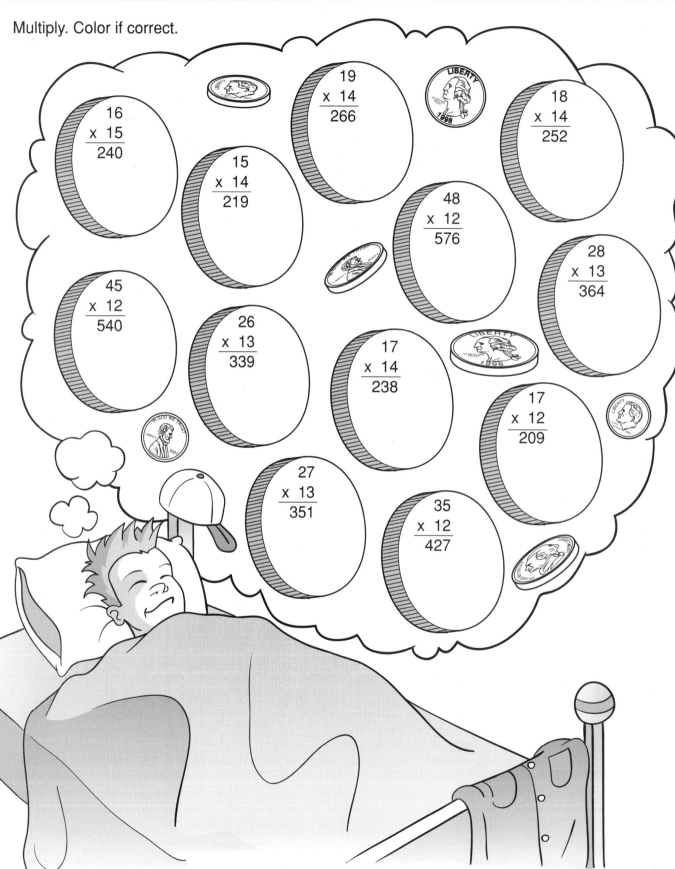

$$\begin{array}{r} 16 \\ \times\ 15 \\ \hline 240 \end{array}$$

$$\begin{array}{r} 19 \\ \times\ 14 \\ \hline 266 \end{array}$$

$$\begin{array}{r} 18 \\ \times\ 14 \\ \hline 252 \end{array}$$

$$\begin{array}{r} 15 \\ \times\ 14 \\ \hline 219 \end{array}$$

$$\begin{array}{r} 48 \\ \times\ 12 \\ \hline 576 \end{array}$$

$$\begin{array}{r} 28 \\ \times\ 13 \\ \hline 364 \end{array}$$

$$\begin{array}{r} 45 \\ \times\ 12 \\ \hline 540 \end{array}$$

$$\begin{array}{r} 26 \\ \times\ 13 \\ \hline 339 \end{array}$$

$$\begin{array}{r} 17 \\ \times\ 14 \\ \hline 238 \end{array}$$

$$\begin{array}{r} 17 \\ \times\ 12 \\ \hline 209 \end{array}$$

$$\begin{array}{r} 27 \\ \times\ 13 \\ \hline 351 \end{array}$$

$$\begin{array}{r} 35 \\ \times\ 12 \\ \hline 427 \end{array}$$

Name _____   Date _____

Burger Barn

Multiply.

G.   45
  x 12
	M. 24
	  x 13
		A. 49
		  x 12
			R. 17
			  x 15
				Y. 37
				  x 13

L.   16
  x 13
	T. 19
	  x 12
		U. 15
		  x 14
			R. 16
			  x 14	

A.   15
  x 15
	S. 63
	  x 13
		R. 17
		  x 13		

B.   37
  x 12
	G. 16
	  x 15
		E. 24
		  x 23		

What type of security system do fast food places use?
To solve the riddle, write each letter from above on its matching numbered line below.
Not all letters will be used.

___ ___ ___ ___ ___ ___   ___ ___ ___ ___ ___ ___
444 210 255 540 552 224   225 208 588 221 312 819

Name _____ Date _____

"Toad"

Solve.

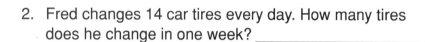

1. Fred tows 16 cars each day. He tows the same number of cars for 15 days. How many cars does he tow in all? _____

2. Fred changes 14 car tires every day. How many tires does he change in one week? _____

3. Twelve cars each have a broken headlight. It takes Fred 23 minutes to change each headlight. How many minutes does it take Fred to change all the headlights?

   _____

4. Fred works 40 hours every week. How many hours does he work in 52 weeks? _____

5. Fourteen mechanics work for Fred. Each mechanic works on 25 cars a day. How many cars in all do the mechanics work on each day? _____

6. Fred receives 16 phone calls. He spends 13 minutes answering each call. How long is Fred on the phone? _____

Name _____

Date _____

Prairie Dog Passage

Multiply to find your way through the prairie tunnel.

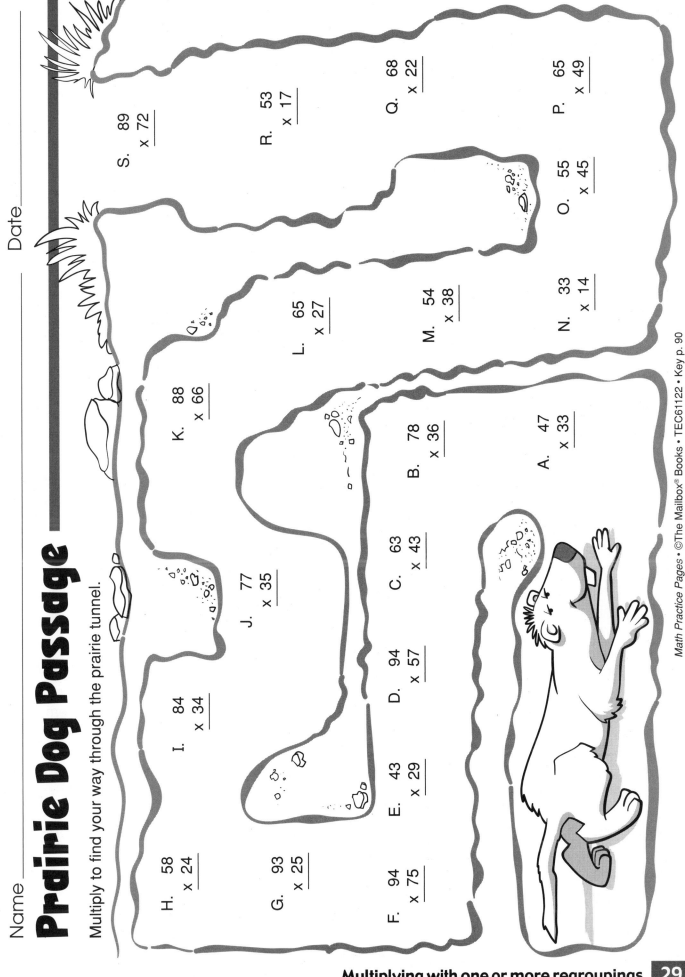

S. 89
x 72

R. 53
x 17

Q. 68
x 22

P. 65
x 49

O. 55
x 45

L. 65
x 27

M. 54
x 38

N. 33
x 14

K. 88
x 66

B. 78
x 36

A. 47
x 33

J. 77
x 35

C. 63
x 43

D. 94
x 57

I. 84
x 34

E. 43
x 29

H. 58
x 24

G. 93
x 25

F. 94
x 75

Multiplying with one or more regroupings

Name _____   Date _____

The Boss

Multiply.

A.   83
   x 25

B.   53
   x 27

C.   68
   x 38

D.   84
   x 56

E.   45
   x 39

F.   95
   x 17

H.   94
   x 67

I.   72
   x 28

O.   63
   x 46

R.   58
   x 34

S.   75
   x 66

T.   59
   x 42

U.   73
   x 24

V.   67
   x 13

Y.   86
   x 36

Why do dragons make poor managers?
To solve the riddle, write each letter from
above on its matching numbered line below.

___ ___ ___ ___ ___ ___ ___
1,431 1,755 2,584 2,075 1,752 4,950 1,755

___ ___ ___ ___   ___ ___ ___ ___
2,478 6,298 1,755 3,096   1,615 2,016 1,972 1,755

___ ___ ___ ___   ___ ___ ___ ___ ___!
1,755 871 1,755 1,972   3,096 1,431 2,898 4,704 3,096

Name _____ Date _____

Treasure Trove

Multiply.

A. 78 x 33	B. 56 x 43	C. 77 x 36	D. 65 x 18

E. 48 x 29	F. 92 x 89	G. 65 x 19	H. 94 x 59

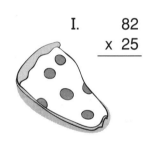

I. 82 x 25	J. 65 x 29	K. 78 x 44

L. 23 x 18	M. 47 x 32	N. 96 x 75	O. 44 x 37	P. 77 x 54

Q. 95 x 92	R. 55 x 46	S. 69 x 22	T. 78 x 63

Name _____   Date _____

Too Cool ━━━━━━━━━━━━━━━━━━━━━━

Solve.

1. Tim owns a store called 2 Cool 4 U. He ordered 38 boxes of posters. If each box has 26 posters, how many posters did Tim order in all?

2. Tim's brother Jim wants to buy 32 large boxes of video games. There are 25 video games in each box. How many video games does Jim want to buy?

3. Tim receives 36 boxes of broken sunglasses, which he'll have to return. There are 24 sunglasses in each box. How many sunglasses will Tim have to send back?

4. Tim sets up a display of cool lamps. There are 48 lamps in each row. There are 35 rows of lamps. How many lamps does Tim put on display?

5. Tim and Jim buy 25 cases of cool jewelry. There are 15 pieces of jewelry in each case. How many pieces of jewelry do Tim and Jim buy?

6. Jim has sold out of the latest toy and needs to order more. There are 52 toys in each box. If Jim orders 18 boxes, how many toys is he ordering?

Name _____   Date _____

To the Rescue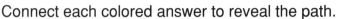

Divide.
Color each correct answer.
Connect each colored answer to reveal the path.

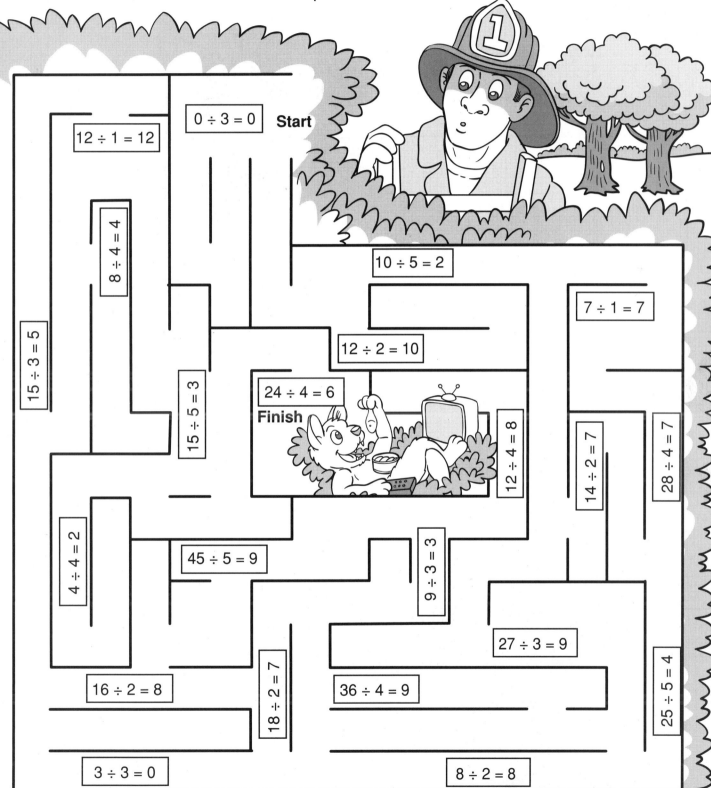

0 ÷ 3 = 0   **Start**

12 ÷ 1 = 12

8 ÷ 4 = 4

15 ÷ 3 = 5

15 ÷ 5 = 3

10 ÷ 5 = 2

7 ÷ 1 = 7

12 ÷ 2 = 10

24 ÷ 4 = 6

Finish

12 ÷ 4 = 8

14 ÷ 2 = 7

28 ÷ 4 = 7

4 ÷ 4 = 2

45 ÷ 5 = 9

9 ÷ 3 = 3

27 ÷ 3 = 9

25 ÷ 5 = 4

16 ÷ 2 = 8

18 ÷ 2 = 7

36 ÷ 4 = 9

3 ÷ 3 = 0

8 ÷ 2 = 8

Math Practice Pages • ©The Mailbox® Books • TEC61122 • Key p. 90

Basic division facts: 0–5   33

"Purr-fect"

Divide.

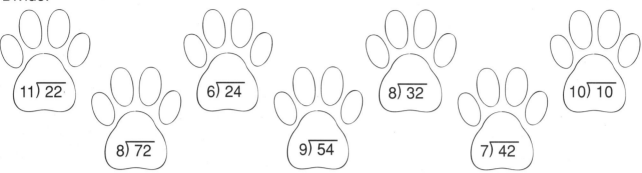

$11\overline{)22}$ $6\overline{)24}$ $8\overline{)32}$ $10\overline{)10}$

$8\overline{)72}$ $9\overline{)54}$ $7\overline{)42}$

M. $10\overline{)70}$ O. $6\overline{)0}$ N. $12\overline{)12}$ R. $8\overline{)48}$ S. $12\overline{)48}$

T. $9\overline{)18}$ I. $10\overline{)30}$

U. $10\overline{)100}$ A. $9\overline{)45}$

C. $12\overline{)132}$ E. $10\overline{)90}$

B. $12\overline{)144}$ T. $12\overline{)96}$

Why did the cat put the letter _M_ in the freezer?

To solve the riddle, write each letter from above on its matching numbered line or lines below.

___ ___ ___ ___ ___ ___ ___   ___ ___   ___ ___ ___ ___ ___
12   9   11   5   10   4   9   3   2   2   10   6   1   4

___ ___ ___   ___ ___ ___ ___   ___ ___ ___ ___!
3   11   9   3   1   8   0   7   3   11   9

To the Pyramids

Use patterns to find each quotient.

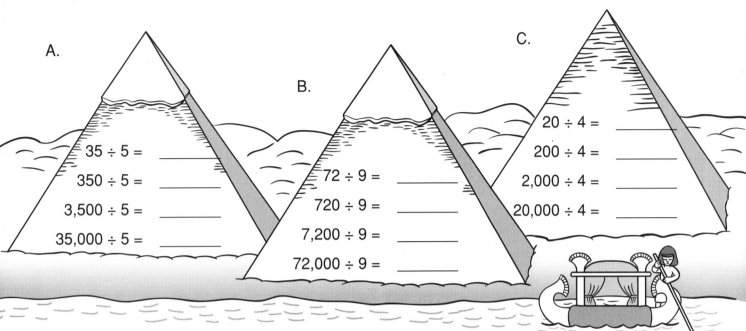

A.

$35 ÷ 5 =$ _____

$350 ÷ 5 =$ _____

$3,500 ÷ 5 =$ _____

$35,000 ÷ 5 =$ _____

B.

$72 ÷ 9 =$ _____

$720 ÷ 9 =$ _____

$7,200 ÷ 9 =$ _____

$72,000 ÷ 9 =$ _____

C.

$20 ÷ 4 =$ _____

$200 ÷ 4 =$ _____

$2,000 ÷ 4 =$ _____

$20,000 ÷ 4 =$ _____

Use mental math to find each quotient.

D. $180 ÷ 2 =$ E. $360 ÷ 4 =$ F. $10,000 ÷ 2 =$ G. $1,500 ÷ 3 =$

H. $140 ÷ 2 =$ I. $48,000 ÷ 8 =$

J. $560 ÷ 7 =$ K. $100 ÷ 5 =$

L. $210 ÷ 3 =$

M. $2,800 ÷ 7 =$

N. $81,000 ÷ 9 =$

O. $540 ÷ 6 =$

Name _____   Date _____

Water Works

Circle the best estimate.

Cross out each answer below to reveal the answer to the riddle.

136 ÷ 2 =
70   100

578 ÷ 3 =
200   300

241 ÷ 4 =
30   60

385 ÷ 5 =
60   80

783 ÷ 2 =
400   500

825 ÷ 4 =
100   200

416 ÷ 2 =
110   200

423 ÷ 8 =
50   90

121 ÷ 6 =
20   30

667 ÷ 7 =
100   410

252 ÷ 5 =
30   50

862 ÷ 3 =
300   450

What kind of pliers do math students use?

M 10	U 410	A 200	L 280	D 400	T 40	I 220	W 50
P 150	G 50	L 450	C 20	K 70	I 30	H 80	V 60
	B 300	Q 200	E 90	F 100	R 340	N 200	S 130

___ ___ ___ ___ ___ ___ ___ ___

Name _____

Above the Rims

Estimate.
Color the tire with the matching answer.

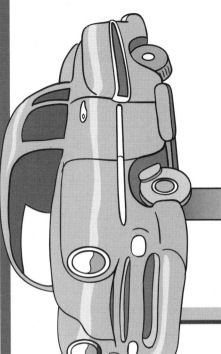

A. 157 ÷ 2 =

B. 318 ÷ 2 =

C. 283 ÷ 4 =

D. 204 ÷ 5 =

E. 175 ÷ 3 =

F. 146 ÷ 5 =

G. 364 ÷ 6 =

H. 182 ÷ 6 =

I. 236 ÷ 3 =

J. 251 ÷ 5 =

K. 453 ÷ 5 =

L. 903 ÷ 9 =

M. 718 ÷ 8 =

N. 238 ÷ 4 =

O. 627 ÷ 9 =

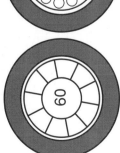

Math Practice Pages • ©The Mailbox® Books • TEC61122 • Key p. 91

Estimating quotients 37

Name _____ Date _____

Goal!

Divide. Color the matching answer.

A. 2)52   B. 8)16   C. 7)63   D. 4)32   E. 2)12

F. 8)72   G. 9)36   H. 6)66   I. 6)42   J. 7)91

K. 5)25   L. 2)74   M. 3)18   N. 3)96   O. 5)85

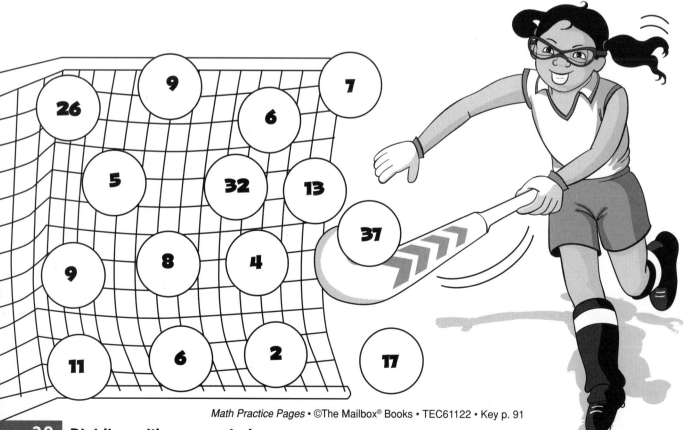

Name _____ Date _____

Quite a Workout!

Divide.

A. 7)‾87‾   B. 3)‾41‾   C. 4)‾74‾

D. 5)‾96‾   E. 6)‾89‾   F. 4)‾55‾   G. 7)‾97‾

H. 2)‾25‾   I. 2)‾43‾   J. 8)‾98‾   K. 3)‾65‾   L. 4)‾61‾

M. 8)‾95‾   N. 5)‾82‾   O. 6)‾93‾

Alien Invasion

Divide.
Color the spaceship with the matching answer.

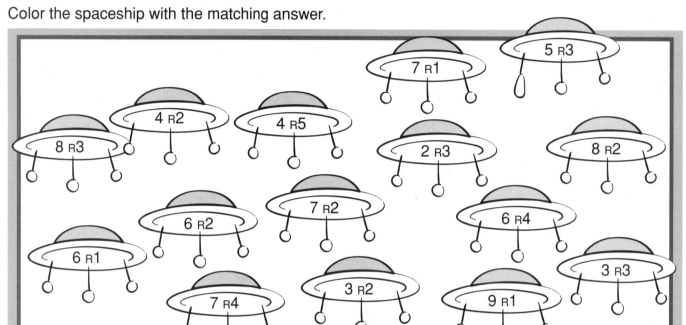

A. 8)66   B. 7)44   C. 8)37   D. 5)34   E. 9)38   F. 7)24

G. 6)51   H. 6)33   I. 5)39

J. 2)19   K. 3)22   L. 2)13

M. 4)30   N. 4)11   O. 6)20

North Pole Numbers

Solve.

1. The polar bear ate 36 fish in four hours. If he ate the same amount each hour, how many fish did he eat in one hour?

2. The polar bear saw 46 seals in the morning. If the seals were to gather in groups of seven, how many groups of seals would there be?

3. The brother and sister polar bears went swimming 24 times in three days. Each day they swam the same number of times. How many times did they swim each day?

4. Sixteen polar bear cubs ate 32 fish. It took them 20 minutes to eat the fish. If each cub ate the same amount of fish, how many fish did each cub eat?

5. The polar bear had a total of 21 snowballs. He divided them into groups of six. How many groups of snowballs did he make?

6. The brother polar bear gave the sister polar bear 58 icicles. She divided the icicles into groups of four. How many groups of icicles did she make?

Name _____ Date _____

Build Your Own Robot

Solve.

1. Mia buys 53 robot kits. She gives each of 9 friends the same number of kits. Mia has 8 robot kits left over. How many kits will each friend get?

2. The Robo-Co factory has 76 elbow springs. They put 8 springs into each box. How many full boxes will Robo-Co have?

3. There are 7 large bins in the Robo-Co factory. There are 62 boxes. If each bin holds an equal number of boxes, how many boxes will not fit into the bins?

4. John buys 4 robot kits. There are a total of 26 parts. If each robot uses the same number of parts, how many extra parts does John have?

5. John ordered 17 robot kits. The delivery man can carry 7 kits at a time. How many trips will the delivery man have to make to unload all the kits?

6. Mia is ordering 46 robot kits. For every 6 kits she orders, she gets a free T-shirt. How many T-shirts will Mia receive?

42

Dividing with remainders

Round the Bases

Divide.

(A) $5\overline{)621}$ (B) $7\overline{)863}$ (C) $4\overline{)858}$ (D) $6\overline{)765}$ (E) $5\overline{)691}$ (F) $3\overline{)413}$

(G) $2\overline{)736}$

(I) $3\overline{)783}$

(H) $9\overline{)999}$

(J) $7\overline{)847}$ (K) $6\overline{)987}$ (L) $4\overline{)893}$ (M) $5\overline{)568}$ (N) $2\overline{)598}$ (O) $8\overline{)896}$

House of Nuts

Divide.
Color the acorn with the matching answer.

A. 8)744   B. 6)378   C. 7)596

D. 4)293   E. 3)268   F. 8)370

G. 2)136   H. 6)526   I. 9)250

J. 5)255   K. 3)171   L. 7)462

M. 5)365   N. 9)328   O. 2)187

89 R1

68   36 R4

73 R1   51   27 R7

93   57   63

73   66

46 R2

87 R4

85 R1

93 R1

Dividing with and without remainders

Stampede!

Name _____   Date _____

Divide.
Color the boxes with remainders to reveal the path.

FINISH

3) 222	2) 158	9) 468	6) 324	9) 729	8) 556
6) 521	4) 253	7) 449	8) 744	3) 144	7) 255
Start		5) 256	6) 285	5) 390	2) 197
		3) 153	7) 659	4) 137	8) 613

Name _____   Date _____

Out West

Divide.
Lasso (circle) all problems in which the remainder is an odd number.

A. $2\overline{)415}$ B. $3\overline{)392}$ C. $6\overline{)651}$ D. $4\overline{)836}$ E. $5\overline{)509}$

F. $7\overline{)773}$ G. $9\overline{)954}$ H. $8\overline{)816}$ I. $4\overline{)429}$

J. $2\overline{)261}$ K. $6\overline{)665}$ L. $3\overline{)615}$

M. $7\overline{)911}$ N. $9\overline{)909}$ O. $5\overline{)701}$

Bright Idea

Divide.

A. 5)532   M. 2)221   H. 2)617   R. 4)443   I. 6)632

N. 7)763   T. 8)812   B. 5)519   E. 6)659   D. 7)724

C. 8)848

S. 9)983

Why was the scientist's hair wet?
To solve the riddle, write each letter from above on its matching numbered
line or lines below.

___ ___ ___ ___ U ___ ___   ___ ___   ___ ___ ___
103 R4 109 R5 106 106 R2   109 R2 109 R5   308 R1 109 R5   308 R1 106 R2 103 R3

___ ___ ___ ___ ___ ___ ___ ___ O ___ ___
106 R2   103 R4 110 R3 106 R2 105 R2 109   109 R2 101 R4   110 R3 110 R1

Name _____ Date _____

Movies 'n' More

Solve.

1. Meg sold 525 movies in five days. She sold the same number of movies each day. How many movies did she sell in one day?	2. Vinny sold 318 video games in three days. He sold the same number of video games each day. How many games did he sell in one day?
3. Meg is boxing 956 movies to store in the warehouse. She can fit seven movies in one box. How many boxes will she need to pack all the movies?	4. Vinny must place two labels on each new video that the store receives. He has 367 labels. How many videos can Vinny label?
5. Eight boxes of videos total 392 pounds. If the weight of each box is equal, how many pounds does one box weigh?	6. Meg sent 306 movies to nine stores in the city. Each store received the same number of movies. How many movies did Meg deliver to one store?

Name _____ Date _____

A Time to Change

Write the fraction for each shaded portion shown.

1.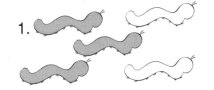

_____

2.

_____

3.

_____

4.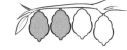

_____

5.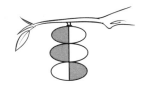

_____

6.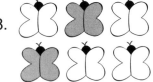

_____

7.

_____

8.

_____

9.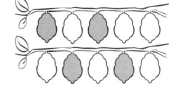

_____

10.

_____

11.

_____

12.

_____

Name _____ Date _____

A Riddle

Circle the equivalent fraction.
To create a riddle, write the letter of each circled fraction on its matching numbered line below.

D $\frac{1}{3}$ =	W $\frac{2}{4}$ =	L $\frac{5}{6}$ =	T $\frac{2}{3}$ =	Y $\frac{3}{5}$ =	K $\frac{10}{12}$ =
$\frac{6}{18}$ $\frac{2}{5}$	$\frac{6}{8}$ $\frac{4}{8}$	$\frac{25}{30}$ $\frac{20}{30}$	$\frac{8}{12}$ $\frac{6}{15}$	$\frac{6}{15}$ $\frac{9}{15}$	$\frac{5}{6}$ $\frac{3}{4}$

P $\frac{3}{8}$ =	M $\frac{6}{7}$ =	H $\frac{5}{8}$ =	A $\frac{2}{4}$ =	O $\frac{4}{6}$ =
$\frac{15}{30}$ $\frac{12}{32}$	$\frac{36}{42}$ $\frac{24}{27}$	$\frac{10}{24}$ $\frac{20}{32}$	$\frac{4}{6}$ $\frac{10}{20}$	$\frac{16}{24}$ $\frac{8}{16}$

B $\frac{2}{5}$ =	E $\frac{1}{2}$ =	U $\frac{3}{4}$ =
$\frac{14}{35}$ $\frac{10}{10}$	$\frac{19}{38}$ $\frac{18}{38}$	$\frac{9}{16}$ $\frac{6}{8}$

S $\frac{7}{8}$ =
$\frac{15}{16}$ $\frac{21}{24}$

It runs all ___ ___ ___ but never ___ ___ ___ ___ ___ .
$\frac{6}{18}$ $\frac{10}{20}$ $\frac{9}{15}$ $\frac{4}{8}$ $\frac{10}{20}$ $\frac{25}{30}$ $\frac{5}{6}$ $\frac{21}{24}$

It often ___ ___ ___ ___ ___ ___ ___ but never ___ ___ ___ ___ ___ .
$\frac{14}{35}$ $\frac{10}{20}$ $\frac{14}{35}$ $\frac{14}{35}$ $\frac{25}{30}$ $\frac{19}{38}$ $\frac{21}{24}$ $\frac{8}{12}$ $\frac{10}{20}$ $\frac{25}{30}$ $\frac{5}{6}$ $\frac{21}{24}$

It has a ___ ___ ___ but never ___ ___ ___ ___ ___ ___ .
$\frac{14}{35}$ $\frac{19}{38}$ $\frac{6}{18}$ $\frac{21}{24}$ $\frac{25}{30}$ $\frac{19}{38}$ $\frac{19}{38}$ $\frac{12}{32}$ $\frac{21}{24}$

It has a ___ ___ ___ ___ ___ but never ___ ___ ___ ___ .
$\frac{36}{42}$ $\frac{16}{24}$ $\frac{6}{8}$ $\frac{8}{12}$ $\frac{20}{32}$ $\frac{19}{38}$ $\frac{10}{20}$ $\frac{8}{12}$ $\frac{21}{24}$

What is it?

_____

Surf's Up

Round each fraction to 0, $\frac{1}{2}$, or 1.
Write the letter of each fraction on its matching surfboard.

A. $\frac{5}{8}$ _____   I. $\frac{11}{12}$ _____   Q. $\frac{11}{18}$ _____

B. $\frac{9}{10}$ _____   J. $\frac{7}{12}$ _____   R. $\frac{4}{5}$ _____

C. $\frac{3}{7}$ _____   K. $\frac{2}{9}$ _____   S. $\frac{3}{5}$ _____

D. $\frac{1}{5}$ _____   L. $\frac{7}{15}$ _____   T. $\frac{1}{7}$ _____

E. $\frac{7}{16}$ _____   M. $\frac{97}{100}$ _____   U. $\frac{9}{20}$ _____

F. $\frac{41}{45}$ _____   N. $\frac{2}{4}$ _____   V. $\frac{7}{8}$ _____

G. $\frac{3}{8}$ _____   O. $\frac{2}{15}$ _____   W. $\frac{4}{10}$ _____

H. $\frac{1}{8}$ _____   P. $\frac{4}{9}$ _____   X. $\frac{1}{10}$ _____

0

$\frac{1}{2}$

1

Weather Humor

Order each set of fractions from least to greatest.
Write the letter of each circled fraction on its matching numbered line or lines below to complete and solve the riddle.

E. $\frac{2}{9}$, $\frac{7}{9}$, $\frac{4}{9}$ ___ , (___) , ___

A. $\frac{4}{5}$, $\frac{3}{5}$, $\frac{2}{5}$ ___ , ___ , (___)

Y. $\frac{3}{7}$, $\frac{5}{7}$, $\frac{2}{7}$ (___) , ___ , ___

G. $\frac{7}{8}$, $\frac{1}{8}$, $\frac{2}{8}$ ___ , ___ , (___)

R. $\frac{7}{10}$, $\frac{3}{10}$, $\frac{1}{10}$ ___ , (___) , ___

F. $\frac{7}{16}$, $\frac{3}{16}$, $\frac{11}{16}$ (___) , ___ , ___

M. $\frac{5}{12}$, $\frac{1}{12}$, $\frac{11}{12}$ ___ , (___) , ___

W. $\frac{14}{15}$, $\frac{1}{15}$, $\frac{4}{15}$ ___ , ___ , (___)

I. $\frac{7}{11}$, $\frac{5}{11}$, $\frac{2}{11}$ (___) , ___ , ___

S. $\frac{2}{3}$, $\frac{1}{3}$, $\frac{3}{3}$ ___ , (___) , ___

P. $\frac{9}{14}$, $\frac{7}{14}$, $\frac{3}{14}$ (___) , ___ , ___

L. $\frac{10}{20}$, $\frac{18}{20}$, $\frac{8}{20}$ ___ , ___ , (___)

M. $\frac{1}{25}$, $\frac{18}{25}$, $\frac{10}{25}$ ___ , (___) , ___

S. $\frac{3}{4}$, $\frac{1}{4}$, $\frac{2}{4}$ (___) , ___ , ___

O. $\frac{25}{50}$, $\frac{15}{50}$, $\frac{5}{50}$ ___ , ___ , (___)

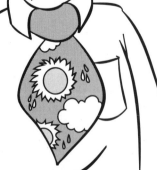

If $\frac{}{\frac{4}{5}}$ $\frac{}{\frac{3}{14}}$ $\frac{}{\frac{3}{10}}$ $\frac{}{\frac{2}{11}}$ $\frac{}{\frac{18}{20}}$ showers bring $\frac{}{\frac{5}{12}}$ $\frac{}{\frac{4}{5}}$ $\frac{}{\frac{2}{7}}$ flowers,

then what do May $\frac{}{\frac{3}{16}}$ $\frac{}{\frac{18}{20}}$ $\frac{}{\frac{25}{50}}$ $\frac{}{\frac{14}{15}}$ $\frac{}{\frac{4}{9}}$ $\frac{}{\frac{3}{10}}$ $\frac{}{\frac{2}{3}}$ bring?

$\frac{}{\frac{3}{14}}$ $\frac{}{\frac{2}{11}}$ $\frac{}{\frac{18}{20}}$ $\frac{}{\frac{7}{8}}$ $\frac{}{\frac{3}{10}}$ $\frac{}{\frac{2}{11}}$ $\frac{}{\frac{10}{25}}$ $\frac{}{\frac{1}{4}}$!

Pigeon to the Rescue

Rewrite each set of fractions in order from least to greatest.
Color if correct to reveal the path.

$\frac{1}{4}, \frac{1}{2}, \frac{5}{6}$

_____

$\frac{1}{6}, \frac{1}{8}, \frac{2}{3}$

_____

$\frac{7}{8}, \frac{2}{9}, \frac{1}{3}$

_____

$\frac{1}{6}, \frac{2}{9}, \frac{1}{3}$

_____

$\frac{1}{2}, \frac{1}{8}, \frac{1}{7}$

_____

$\frac{4}{5}, \frac{9}{10}, \frac{11}{12}$

_____

$\frac{3}{7}, \frac{1}{2}, \frac{3}{4}$

_____

$\frac{3}{10}, \frac{2}{3}, \frac{4}{5}$

_____

$\frac{2}{3}, \frac{5}{7}, \frac{7}{9}$

_____

$\frac{7}{12}, \frac{3}{10}, \frac{1}{5}$

_____

$\frac{3}{8}, \frac{9}{10}, \frac{1}{4}$

_____

$\frac{3}{4}, \frac{1}{2}, \frac{11}{16}$

_____

$\frac{1}{3}, \frac{2}{5}, \frac{1}{2}$

_____

$\frac{6}{7}, \frac{2}{3}, \frac{5}{6}$

_____

$\frac{1}{3}, \frac{5}{9}, \frac{7}{18}$

_____

$\frac{5}{8}, \frac{7}{16}, \frac{3}{4}$

_____

$\frac{3}{8}, \frac{3}{5}, \frac{7}{10}$

_____

$\frac{1}{6}, \frac{1}{5}, \frac{2}{9}$

_____

$\frac{3}{4}, \frac{2}{5}, \frac{13}{16}$

_____

$\frac{9}{14}, \frac{4}{7}, \frac{3}{4}$

_____

Math Practice Pages • ©The Mailbox® Books • TEC61122 • Key p. 93

Ordering fractions 53

Jumping Through Hoops

List the first 9 multiples for each number. Then circle the least common multiple in each pair.

A. | 3 | |
C. | 7 | |

B. | 2 | |
D. | 3 | |
  | 5 | |
  | 8 | |

A. row: | 3 |
C. row: | 7 |
(below) 4 / 9

E. | 2 | |
  | 4 | |

G. | 4 | |
  | 5 | |

F. | 3 | |
  | 9 | |

H. | 2 | |
  | 6 | |

I. | 9 | |
  | 4 | |

K. | 6 | |
  | 8 | |

J. | 12 | |
  | 3 | |

L. | 2 | |
  | 7 | |

Least common multiples

Math Practice Pages • ©The Mailbox® Books • TEC61122 • Key p. 93

Name _____ Date _____

Special Agents

Lightly color the greatest common factor in each row. The first one has been done for you.

1.	3 and 6	K 1	W 2	**L 3**	J 6
2.	4 and 8	D 4	O 2	C 1	I 8
3.	10 and 20	F 5	A 10	X 20	H 2
4.	16 and 32	U 4	O 16	R 8	G 2
5.	6 and 12	H 3	S 4	R 6	F 12
6.	4 and 14	A 1	E 4	V 7	T 2
7.	28 and 35	M 2	T 4	K 5	S 7
8.	18 and 27	N 3	B 9	W 1	E 27
9.	5 and 10	E 5	G 10	X 1	A 15
10.	2 and 28	D 1	S 7	G 2	M 6

11.	12 and 32	Q 2	M 4	E 3	A 8
12.	3 and 18	I 6	Y 2	A 3	B 9
13.	7 and 63	D 1	P 9	O 21	N 7
14.	25 and 65	V 5	T 25	D 1	J 13
15.	6 and 14	J 3	I 2	Z 7	Q 6
16.	8 and 28	P 2	L 7	H 4	C 8
17.	15 and 36	B 1	C 6	V 5	E 3
18.	4 and 32	L 2	U 1	R 4	I 16
19.	20 and 80	P 20	F 2	Y 4	N 10
20.	17 and 34	B 1	S 17	R 2	Z 34

What three types of dogs are currently used as part of the CIA K-9 Corps?
To find out, write each shaded letter above its matching problem number.

$\underline{L}$ $\underline{}$ $\underline{}$ $\underline{}$ $\underline{}$ $\underline{}$ $\underline{}$ $\underline{}$ $\underline{}$ $\underline{}$ $\underline{}$ $\underline{}$ $\underline{}$ $\underline{}$ $\underline{}$ $\underline{}$ $\underline{}$ $\underline{}$,
1 3 8 18 12 2 4 5   18 9 6 5 15 17 14 9 18 20

$\underline{}$ $\underline{}$ $\underline{}$ $\underline{}$ $\underline{}$ $\underline{}$ $\underline{}$ $\underline{}$ $\underline{}$ $\underline{}$ $\underline{}$ $\underline{}$ $\underline{}$ $\underline{}$, and
10 9 5 11 12 13   7 16 17 19 16 9 5 2 20

$\underline{}$ $\underline{}$ $\underline{L}$ $\underline{}$ $\underline{}$ $\underline{}$ $\underline{}$ $\underline{}$ $\underline{}$ $\underline{L}$ $\underline{}$ $\underline{}$ $\underline{}$ $\underline{}$ $\underline{}$
8 9 1 10 15 3 13   11 3 1 15 13 4 15 7

On a Mission

Write each fraction in simplest form.
Cross out each matching answer.

A. $\dfrac{2}{4} =$ B. $\dfrac{4}{20} =$

C. $\dfrac{25}{100} =$ D. $\dfrac{3}{6} =$

E. $\dfrac{10}{12} =$ F. $\dfrac{3}{9} =$

G. $\dfrac{4}{8} =$ H. $\dfrac{9}{12} =$ I. $\dfrac{6}{8} =$

J. $\dfrac{10}{25} =$ K. $\dfrac{4}{6} =$ L. $\dfrac{16}{24} =$ M. $\dfrac{14}{35} =$

N. $\dfrac{4}{32} =$ O. $\dfrac{10}{60} =$

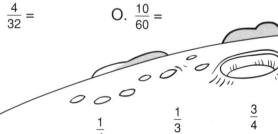

$\dfrac{1}{5}$ $\dfrac{1}{4}$ $\dfrac{1}{3}$ $\dfrac{3}{4}$ $\dfrac{3}{4}$ $\dfrac{2}{5}$ $\dfrac{1}{8}$ $\dfrac{1}{6}$

$\dfrac{5}{6}$ $\dfrac{1}{2}$ $\dfrac{1}{2}$ $\dfrac{1}{2}$ $\dfrac{2}{3}$ $\dfrac{2}{3}$ $\dfrac{2}{5}$

Name _____   Date _____

Vroom!

Change each improper fraction to a mixed or whole number. Change each mixed number to an improper fraction. Reduce fractions as needed. Then cross out the matching answer.

A. $\frac{54}{7}$ =   B. $3\frac{6}{7}$ =   C. $\frac{37}{2}$ =   D. $8\frac{7}{8}$ =   E. $\frac{14}{5}$ =

F. $16\frac{3}{4}$ =   G. $\frac{24}{9}$ =   H. $4\frac{1}{8}$ =   I. $2\frac{1}{2}$ =   J. $14\frac{3}{5}$ =

K. $\frac{49}{7}$ =   L. $3\frac{2}{3}$ =   M. $10\frac{3}{8}$ =   N. $\frac{13}{3}$ =   O. $\frac{58}{10}$ =

P. $\frac{18}{4}$ =   Q. $2\frac{5}{12}$ =   R. $\frac{15}{8}$ =   S. $\frac{72}{9}$ =

T. $6\frac{4}{5}$ =

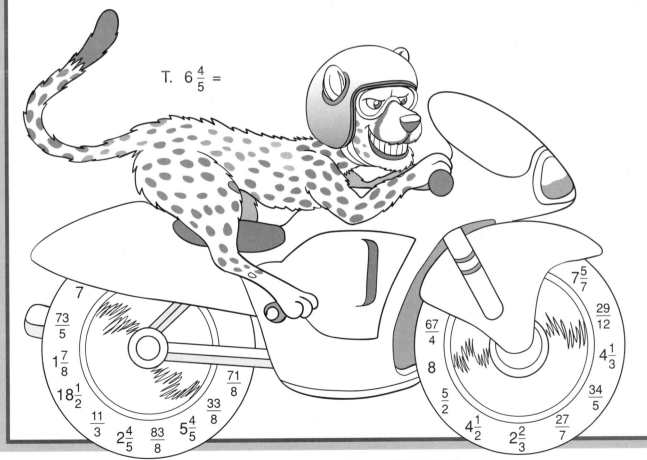

Math Practice Pages • ©The Mailbox® Books • TEC61122 • Key p. 93

On the Track

Add.
Write each answer in its simplest form.
Cross out each matching answer. Not all fractions will be crossed out.

A. $\frac{1}{4} + \frac{2}{4} =$

B. $\frac{1}{13} + \frac{3}{13} =$

C. $\frac{1}{7} + \frac{4}{7} =$

D. $\frac{3}{5} + \frac{1}{5} =$

E. $\frac{2}{9} + \frac{5}{9} =$

F. $\frac{1}{3} + \frac{1}{3} =$

G. $\frac{2}{5} + \frac{1}{5} =$

H. $\frac{3}{8} + \frac{5}{8} =$

I. $\frac{2}{7} + \frac{4}{7} =$

J. $\frac{10}{21} + \frac{6}{21} =$

K. $\frac{3}{11} + \frac{5}{11} =$

L. $\frac{7}{17} + \frac{5}{17} =$

$\frac{3}{4}$　$\frac{8}{11}$　$\frac{2}{3}$　$\frac{5}{7}$

$\frac{16}{21}$　$\frac{4}{13}$　$\frac{7}{9}$　$\frac{12}{17}$

$\frac{4}{5}$　$\frac{3}{5}$　$\frac{7}{8}$　$\frac{2}{5}$

1　$\frac{6}{7}$

Adding fractions

Math Practice Pages • ©The Mailbox® Books • TEC61122 • Key p. 93

Name _____   Date _____

Make It Snappy

Subtract.

A. $\dfrac{7}{11}$ $-\dfrac{3}{11}$ B. $\dfrac{2}{3}$ $-\dfrac{1}{3}$ C. $\dfrac{4}{5}$ $-\dfrac{2}{5}$ D. $\dfrac{8}{17}$ $-\dfrac{4}{17}$ E. $\dfrac{10}{21}$ $-\dfrac{8}{21}$

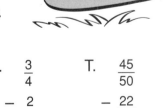

F. $\dfrac{3}{5}$ $-\dfrac{2}{5}$ G. $\dfrac{7}{9}$ $-\dfrac{5}{9}$ H. $\dfrac{6}{7}$ $-\dfrac{2}{7}$ I. $\dfrac{14}{15}$ $-\dfrac{1}{15}$

J. $\dfrac{17}{19}$ $-\dfrac{5}{19}$ K. $\dfrac{15}{23}$ $-\dfrac{5}{23}$ L. $\dfrac{5}{7}$ $-\dfrac{2}{7}$ M. $\dfrac{8}{9}$ $-\dfrac{4}{9}$

N. $\dfrac{10}{11}$ $-\dfrac{3}{11}$ O. $\dfrac{6}{7}$ $-\dfrac{1}{7}$ P. $\dfrac{13}{15}$ $-\dfrac{11}{15}$ Q. $\dfrac{11}{13}$ $-\dfrac{6}{13}$ R. $\dfrac{1}{2}$ $-\dfrac{1}{2}$ S. $\dfrac{3}{4}$ $-\dfrac{2}{4}$ T. $\dfrac{45}{50}$ $-\dfrac{22}{50}$

Name _____ Date _____

Rock Lobster ▬▬▬▬▬▬▬

Solve.

Write your answer in its simplest form.

Color the musical note of each problem that did not need to be simplified.

Ⓐ $\frac{2}{5} + \frac{1}{5} =$ Ⓑ $\frac{3}{5} - \frac{1}{5} =$ Ⓒ $\frac{3}{4} - \frac{1}{4} =$

Ⓓ $\frac{5}{9} + \frac{1}{9} =$ Ⓔ $\frac{8}{15} - \frac{2}{15} =$ Ⓕ $\frac{5}{12} + \frac{5}{12} =$

Ⓖ $\frac{1}{3} + \frac{1}{3} =$ Ⓗ $\frac{5}{6} - \frac{1}{6} =$ Ⓘ $\frac{3}{8} + \frac{5}{8} =$

Ⓙ $\frac{8}{9} - \frac{2}{9} =$ Ⓚ $\frac{3}{14} - \frac{1}{14} =$ Ⓛ $\frac{3}{10} + \frac{7}{10} =$

Ⓜ $\frac{9}{14} - \frac{5}{14} =$ Ⓝ $\frac{4}{11} + \frac{6}{11} =$

Ⓞ $\frac{2}{3} - \frac{1}{3} =$ Ⓟ $\frac{6}{15} + \frac{4}{15} =$

Ⓠ $\frac{2}{7} + \frac{4}{7} =$ Ⓡ $\frac{5}{12} - \frac{1}{12} =$

Ⓢ $\frac{4}{5} - \frac{2}{5} =$ Ⓣ $\frac{1}{3} + \frac{2}{3} =$

Going Buggy

Solve.
If the answer is correct, color the box to reveal the path.

$\frac{1}{6} + \frac{5}{6} = \frac{2}{3}$	$\frac{4}{15} + \frac{9}{15} = \frac{3}{5}$	$\frac{3}{5} - \frac{1}{5} = \frac{2}{5}$
$\frac{5}{8} - \frac{1}{8} = \frac{6}{8}$	$\frac{4}{7} - \frac{2}{7} = \frac{1}{7}$	$\frac{1}{4} + \frac{3}{4} = 1$
$\frac{5}{14} + \frac{3}{14} = \frac{5}{7}$	$\frac{7}{20} + \frac{3}{20} = \frac{1}{2}$	$\frac{7}{8} - \frac{1}{8} = \frac{3}{4}$
$\frac{3}{5} - \frac{1}{5} = \frac{1}{5}$	$\frac{3}{8} + \frac{3}{8} = \frac{3}{4}$	$\frac{9}{10} - \frac{7}{10} = \frac{2}{5}$
$\frac{7}{12} - \frac{5}{12} = \frac{1}{6}$	$\frac{5}{6} - \frac{1}{6} = \frac{1}{2}$	$\frac{5}{16} + \frac{7}{16} = \frac{2}{3}$
$\frac{10}{21} - \frac{4}{21} = \frac{2}{7}$	$\frac{2}{9} + \frac{4}{9} = \frac{2}{3}$	$\frac{3}{5} + \frac{1}{5} = \frac{3}{4}$

Name _____ Date _____

School Daze

Solve.
Write each answer in its simplest form.

1. By 8:00 AM, $\frac{1}{8}$ of the class has arrived. By 8:15 AM, another $\frac{5}{8}$ has arrived. What fraction of the class has arrived by 8:15 AM?

2. In Ms. Martin's fourth-grade class, $\frac{3}{7}$ of the students always write with pencils. Another $\frac{4}{7}$ of the students always write with pens. What fraction of the class always writes with either pencils or pens?

3. Of all the students, $\frac{1}{10}$ of them walk to school. Another $\frac{7}{10}$ of the students ride bikes to school. What fraction of the students walk or ride bikes to school?

4. After the first grading period, $\frac{1}{4}$ of the class was on the A honor roll. Another $\frac{1}{4}$ of the class was on the A-B honor roll. What fraction of the class was on an honor roll?

5. Students spend $\frac{2}{5}$ of the school day working math problems. They spend $\frac{1}{5}$ of the day writing. What fraction of the day do students work math problems and write?

6. When doing homework, $\frac{2}{3}$ of the class finishes at home. Another $\frac{1}{3}$ finishes its homework in the morning. What fraction of the class finishes its homework?

Math Practice Pages • ©The Mailbox® Books • TEC61122 • Key p. 94

Pizza Palace

Solve.
Write each answer in its simplest form.

1. On Andy's pizza, $\frac{3}{4}$ is covered in olives. Andy eats $\frac{1}{4}$ of the olive-covered pieces. What fraction of pizza covered in olives is still left?

2. Pete buys a pepperoni pizza. He eats $\frac{2}{9}$ of it. How much pizza is left?

3. Nikki's parents buy a large cheese pizza and garlic bread. After dinner, $\frac{1}{10}$ of the pizza is left. How much pizza do Nikki and her parents eat?

4. At the pizza buffet, $\frac{2}{3}$ of the pizzas are piping hot. The rest of the pizzas are room temperature. What fraction of the pizzas are room temperature?

5. Andy eats $\frac{2}{5}$ of a sausage pizza for breakfast. He eats the rest of the pizza for lunch. How much pizza does Andy eat for lunch?

6. Pete uses $\frac{5}{12}$ of his pizza sauce on Friday. He uses the rest of the sauce on Saturday. How much sauce does he use on Saturday?

A Weighty Topic

Add.
Write each answer in its simplest form. Then complete the riddle by matching each letter to its numbered line or lines below.

B. $2\frac{1}{4}$
  $+\,4\frac{1}{4}$

O. $3\frac{5}{8}$
  $+\,6\frac{1}{8}$

N. $5\frac{2}{3}$
  $+\,8\frac{1}{3}$

A. $1\frac{4}{7}$
  $+\,9\frac{2}{7}$

D. $7\frac{1}{5}$
  $+\,2\frac{4}{5}$

I. $8\frac{3}{10}$
  $+\,3\frac{1}{10}$

Y. $2\frac{1}{6}$
  $+\,6\frac{1}{6}$

R. $4\frac{5}{9}$
  $+\,1\frac{7}{9}$

C. $9\frac{1}{2}$
  $+\,7\frac{1}{2}$

M. $6\frac{3}{4}$
  $+\,5\frac{3}{4}$

T. $1\frac{7}{10}$
  $+\,9\frac{3}{10}$

V. $7\frac{2}{3}$
  $+\,8\frac{2}{3}$

K. $2\frac{2}{5}$
  $+\,4\frac{4}{5}$

W. $3\frac{4}{7}$
  $+\,5\frac{1}{7}$

H. $2\frac{3}{8}$
  $+\,2\frac{7}{8}$

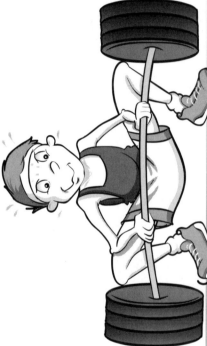

Riddle: F $\overline{}$ $\overline{9\frac{3}{4}}$ $\overline{6\frac{1}{3}}$ $\overline{8\frac{5}{7}}$ $\overline{10\frac{6}{7}}$ $\overline{6\frac{1}{3}}$ $\overline{11\frac{2}{5}}$ $\overline{10\frac{6}{7}}$ $\overline{12\frac{1}{2}}$ $\overline{10\frac{6}{7}}$ $\overline{5\frac{1}{4}}$

$\overline{6\frac{1}{2}}$ $\overline{10\frac{6}{7}}$ $\overline{17}$ $\overline{7\frac{1}{5}}$ $\overline{8\frac{5}{7}}$ $\overline{10\frac{6}{7}}$ $\overline{6\frac{1}{3}}$ $\overline{10}$ $\overline{12\frac{1}{2}}$ $\overline{10\frac{6}{7}}$ $\overline{16\frac{1}{3}}$ $\overline{8\frac{1}{3}}$;

$\overline{11}$ $\overline{9\frac{3}{4}}$ $\overline{11\frac{2}{5}}$ $\overline{10\frac{6}{7}}$ $\overline{11}$ $\overline{12\frac{1}{2}}$ $\overline{9\frac{3}{4}}$ $\overline{11}$.

E $\overline{}$ $\overline{5\frac{1}{4}}$ $\overline{10\frac{6}{7}}$ $\overline{14}$ $\overline{11\frac{2}{5}}$ $\overline{11}$?

Answer: $\overline{10\frac{6}{7}}$ $\overline{14}$ $\overline{8\frac{5}{7}}$ $\overline{11\frac{2}{5}}$

Adding mixed numbers

After "Ewe"

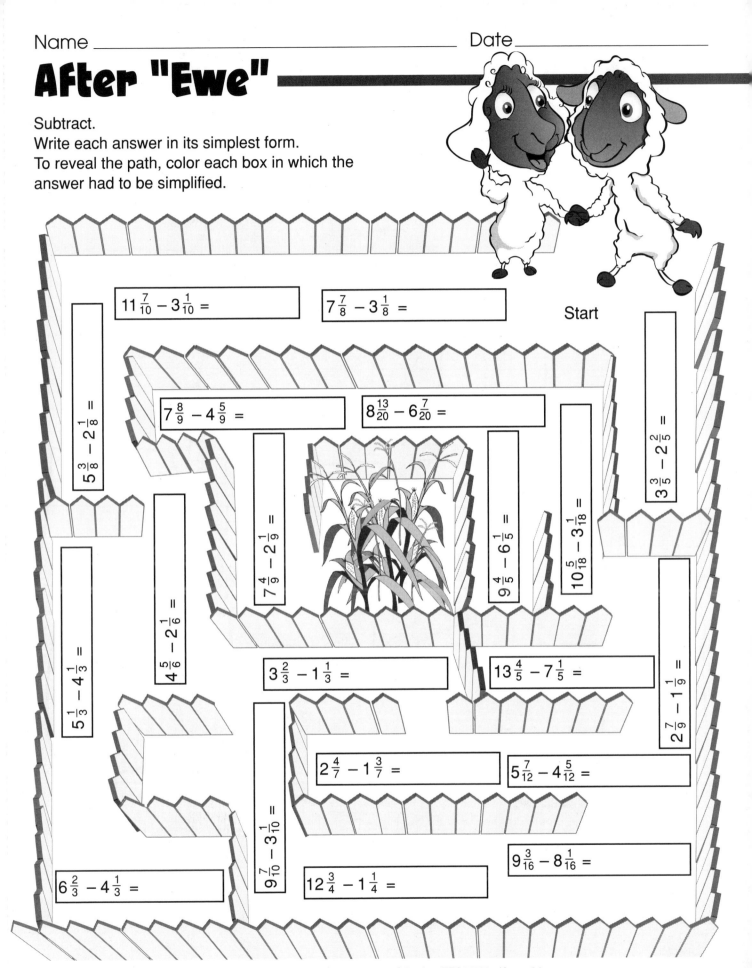

Subtract.
Write each answer in its simplest form.
To reveal the path, color each box in which the
answer had to be simplified.

$11\frac{7}{10} - 3\frac{1}{10} =$

$7\frac{7}{8} - 3\frac{1}{8} =$

Start

$5\frac{3}{8} - 2\frac{1}{8} =$

$7\frac{8}{9} - 4\frac{5}{9} =$

$8\frac{13}{20} - 6\frac{7}{20} =$

$3\frac{3}{5} - 2\frac{2}{5} =$

$7\frac{4}{9} - 2\frac{1}{9} =$

$9\frac{4}{5} - 6\frac{1}{5} =$

$10\frac{5}{18} - 3\frac{1}{18} =$

$5\frac{1}{3} - 4\frac{1}{3} =$

$4\frac{5}{6} - 2\frac{1}{6} =$

$3\frac{2}{3} - 1\frac{1}{3} =$

$13\frac{4}{5} - 7\frac{1}{5} =$

$2\frac{7}{9} - 1\frac{1}{9} =$

$2\frac{4}{7} - 1\frac{3}{7} =$

$5\frac{7}{12} - 4\frac{5}{12} =$

$9\frac{7}{10} - 3\frac{1}{10} =$

$9\frac{3}{16} - 8\frac{1}{16} =$

$6\frac{2}{3} - 4\frac{1}{3} =$

$12\frac{3}{4} - 1\frac{1}{4} =$

A Little Snack

Solve.
Color if correct.

$$12\frac{3}{4}$$
$$-\ 2\frac{1}{4}$$
$$\overline{\ \ 10\frac{1}{2}}$$

$$2\frac{1}{3}$$
$$+\ 6\frac{2}{3}$$
$$\overline{\ \ 9\frac{1}{3}}$$

$$6\frac{4}{7} - 3\frac{2}{7} = 3\frac{2}{7}$$

$$6\frac{3}{10}$$
$$+\ 7\frac{7}{10}$$
$$\overline{\ \ 15}$$

$$5\frac{5}{9} + 8\frac{3}{9} = 15\frac{4}{9}$$

$$7\frac{4}{9}$$
$$-\ 3\frac{2}{9}$$
$$\overline{\ \ 4\frac{1}{3}}$$

$$4\frac{2}{5}$$
$$+\ 1\frac{4}{5}$$
$$\overline{\ \ 6\frac{1}{5}}$$

$$11\frac{7}{12}$$
$$-\ 4\frac{1}{12}$$
$$\overline{\ \ 7\frac{3}{4}}$$

$$17\frac{3}{8}$$
$$-\ 6\frac{1}{8}$$
$$\overline{\ \ 11\frac{1}{4}}$$

$$5\frac{7}{15}$$
$$-\ 3\frac{2}{15}$$
$$\overline{\ \ 8\frac{1}{4}}$$

$$20\frac{4}{7}$$
$$+\ 9\frac{2}{7}$$
$$\overline{\ \ 29\frac{6}{7}}$$

$$15\frac{5}{6}$$
$$-\ 14\frac{1}{6}$$
$$\overline{\ \ 1\frac{1}{3}}$$

$$9\frac{7}{10}$$
$$-\ 1\frac{1}{10}$$
$$\overline{\ \ 10\frac{3}{5}}$$

$$9\frac{3}{5} + 2\frac{2}{5} = 12$$

$$12\frac{7}{9}$$
$$-\ 5\frac{1}{9}$$
$$\overline{\ \ 7\frac{2}{3}}$$

Tools of the Trade

Solve.
Write each answer in its simplest form.
Color the matching answer to reveal the path to the doctor's favorite tool.

A. $11\frac{11}{12} - 4\frac{5}{12} =$	$15\frac{1}{2}$	$7\frac{1}{2}$	$6\frac{6}{12}$	$7\frac{6}{12}$
B. $12\frac{3}{4} + 5\frac{1}{4} =$	$17\frac{1}{2}$	18	$18\frac{1}{2}$	17
C. $6\frac{4}{7} + 7\frac{6}{7} =$	$14\frac{3}{7}$	$13\frac{2}{7}$	$14\frac{1}{2}$	$1\frac{3}{7}$
D. $8\frac{9}{14} - 3\frac{1}{14} =$	$5\frac{4}{7}$	$11\frac{4}{7}$	$8\frac{8}{14}$	$8\frac{1}{2}$
E. $11\frac{2}{9} - 4\frac{1}{9} =$	$6\frac{1}{9}$	$7\frac{1}{9}$	$15\frac{1}{9}$	$3\frac{3}{9}$
F. $2\frac{2}{5} + 1\frac{1}{5} =$	$1\frac{1}{5}$	$1\frac{3}{5}$	$3\frac{3}{5}$	$3\frac{1}{5}$
G. $5\frac{17}{20} - 3\frac{13}{20} =$	$2\frac{4}{20}$	$2\frac{6}{20}$	$2\frac{1}{5}$	$2\frac{1}{2}$
H. $9\frac{3}{5} + 7\frac{1}{5} =$	17	$16\frac{1}{2}$	$16\frac{4}{5}$	$15\frac{5}{6}$
I. $17\frac{7}{8} - 12\frac{5}{8} =$	$29\frac{1}{4}$	$5\frac{1}{4}$	$5\frac{2}{5}$	$5\frac{2}{8}$
J. $9\frac{6}{11} - 4\frac{2}{11} =$	$13\frac{8}{11}$	$5\frac{5}{11}$	$5\frac{4}{11}$	$5\frac{8}{11}$
K. $9\frac{2}{3} + 2\frac{2}{3} =$	$11\frac{4}{5}$	7	$10\frac{1}{3}$	$12\frac{1}{3}$
L. $3\frac{3}{4} - 1\frac{1}{4} =$	$2\frac{2}{4}$	$2\frac{1}{8}$	$2\frac{1}{2}$	$2\frac{2}{8}$
M. $3\frac{1}{4} + 8\frac{3}{4} =$	$11\frac{3}{4}$	12	$7\frac{1}{2}$	$8\frac{1}{4}$
N. $1\frac{3}{5} + 1\frac{4}{5} =$	$2\frac{3}{5}$	$3\frac{2}{5}$	$\frac{2}{5}$	$2\frac{2}{5}$
O. $8\frac{9}{12} - 4\frac{1}{12} =$	$4\frac{8}{12}$	$4\frac{1}{2}$	$4\frac{2}{3}$	$4\frac{5}{6}$

stethoscope	X-ray	lollipops	bandages

Math Practice Pages • ©The Mailbox® Books • TEC61122 • Key p. 94

Adding and subtracting mixed numbers   67

Name _____   Date _____

Big Tex's Diner

Solve.
Write each answer in its simplest form.

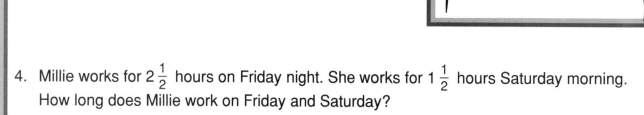

1. Tex is making a pecan pie. He needs $1\frac{4}{8}$ cups of walnuts and $1\frac{2}{8}$ cups of pecans. How many cups of nuts does Tex need in all?

2. Millie is known for her omelets. She uses $2\frac{1}{3}$ cups of cheese and $1\frac{2}{3}$ cups of sausage. How much cheese and sausage does Millie use altogether?

3. Tex puts $2\frac{1}{4}$ cups of onions and $1\frac{3}{4}$ cups of carrots out for the salad bar. How many cups of onions and carrots does Tex put out altogether?

4. Millie works for $2\frac{1}{2}$ hours on Friday night. She works for $1\frac{1}{2}$ hours Saturday morning. How long does Millie work on Friday and Saturday?

5. Tex has $3\frac{2}{8}$ pounds of meat for hamburgers. He buys $1\frac{5}{8}$ more pounds. How much meat does Tex have in all?

6. Tex and Millie use $1\frac{5}{6}$ bags of flour. They also use $2\frac{3}{6}$ bags of sugar. How much flour and sugar do Tex and Millie use in all?

Name _____   Date _____

Juice 'n' Java

Solve.
Write each answer in its simplest form.

1. Jacob is making a fruit smoothie. He has $3\frac{2}{3}$ cups of juice in his measuring cup. If he pours $2\frac{1}{3}$ cups into the blender, how much juice will be left in the cup?

2. To make a large vanilla coffee, Emma adds $1\frac{1}{8}$ teaspoons of vanilla to the coffee. She needs to add a total of $2\frac{3}{8}$ teaspoons. How much more vanilla does she need to add?

3. Jacob washes coffee mugs for $2\frac{3}{4}$ hours each day. If he has already washed mugs for $1\frac{1}{4}$ hours, how much longer does he need to wash mugs?

4. To make a smoothie, Emma adds $7\frac{9}{10}$ ounces of peaches to the mix. She also adds $3\frac{1}{10}$ ounces of berries. How many more ounces of peaches than berries does Emma add?

5. Jacob and Emma are making coffee cake. They need $2\frac{1}{6}$ cups of butter. They add $3\frac{5}{6}$ cups by mistake. How much extra butter did they add?

6. In one week, Jacob and Emma make $4\frac{1}{5}$ gallons of coffee and $10\frac{3}{5}$ gallons of fruit smoothies. How many more gallons of fruit smoothies than coffee does the pair make?

Name _____   Date _____

The Swat Team

Write the decimal and word form for each shaded portion.

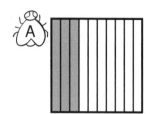 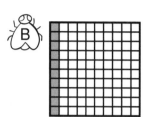

_____   _____
_____   _____

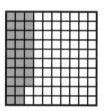 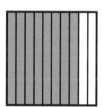 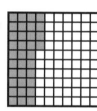

_____   _____   _____   _____
_____   _____   _____   _____

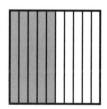 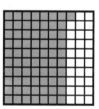 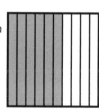 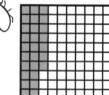

_____   _____   _____   _____
_____   _____   _____   _____

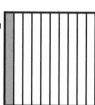 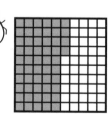

_____   _____
_____   _____

Math Practice Pages • ©The Mailbox® Books • TEC61122 • Key p. 95

70 **Identifying decimals**

Flight Path

Color if correct to reveal the flight path.

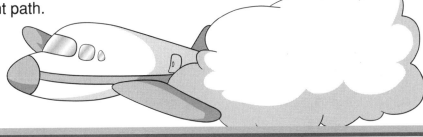

$0.5 = \frac{5}{10}$	$0.29 = \frac{29}{100}$	$0.60 = \frac{6}{100}$	$1.4 = \frac{14}{100}$	$6.03 = 6\frac{3}{10}$
$1.07 = 1\frac{17}{100}$	$0.35 = \frac{35}{100}$	$0.03 = \frac{3}{100}$	$0.2 = \frac{2}{10}$	$0.04 = \frac{4}{10}$
$0.8 = \frac{8}{100}$	$0.5 = \frac{5}{100}$	$2.91 = 2\frac{91}{10}$	$0.6 = \frac{6}{10}$	$4.144 = 4\frac{4}{100}$
$0.9 = \frac{9}{100}$	$5.1 = 5\frac{1}{100}$	$0.81 = \frac{81}{100}$	$0.44 = \frac{44}{100}$	$7.77 = 7\frac{7}{10}$
$3.60 = \frac{36}{100}$	$0.9 = \frac{9}{10}$	$0.35 = \frac{35}{10}$	$8.21 = 8\frac{2}{10}$	$0.05 = \frac{5}{10}$
$0.75 = \frac{75}{100}$	$2.02 = 2\frac{2}{10}$	$0.44 = \frac{44}{10}$	$5.8 = 5\frac{8}{100}$	$8.02 = 8\frac{82}{100}$
$3.09 = 3\frac{9}{10}$	$0.08 = \frac{8}{100}$	$0.16 = \frac{16}{100}$	$1.2 = 1\frac{2}{10}$	$9.11 = 9\frac{11}{10}$
$0.2 = \frac{2}{100}$	$6.4 = 6\frac{4}{100}$	$7.10 = 7\frac{1}{100}$	$9.98 = 9\frac{8}{10}$	$4.05 = 4\frac{5}{100}$

Name _____

Big Plans

Date _____

Color the construction hat for each set of numbers that is in order from least to greatest.
Write each incorrect set of numbers in the correct order.

(A) 0.08
0.9
8.0

(B) 61.73
64.82
64.87
64.99

(C) 17.09
17.90
17.89

(D) 7.68
7.8
8.06
8.7

(E) 5.40
5.41
5.39

(F) 2.31
6.5
9.86

(G) 0.82
0.81
0.80

(H) 0.21
0.27
0.22

(I) 13.94
13.95
14.94

(J) 1.7
1.3
1.0

(K) 5.2
5.17
4.95

(L) 6.53
6.5
6.35
6.30

(M) 45.07
45.57
45.7

(N) 2.01
2.05
2.07

(O) 23.0
57.8
41.03

(P) 18.99
19.10
19.19

Math Practice Pages • ©The Mailbox® Books • TEC61122 • Key p. 95

Comparing and ordering decimals

Name _____ Date _____

Feature Presentation

Round each decimal to the underlined place value.
Cross out each matching answer below. Not all answers will be used.

A. 8.4̲5 =

_____

B. 6̲.9 =

_____

C. 13.0̲1 =

_____

D. 914̲.7 =

_____

E. 100.1̲2 =

_____

F. 6̲8.5 =

_____

G. 49.6̲1 =

_____

H. 69̲.9 =

_____

I. 89.4̲4 =

_____

J. 27̲.50 =

_____

K. 5̲5.2 =

_____

L. 77̲.7 =

_____

M. 104̲.3 =

_____

N. 258̲.6 =

_____

O. 31.8̲8 =

_____

P. 59.6̲2 =

_____

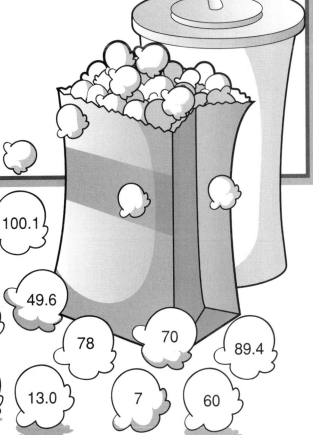

9.5   259   25.8   8.5   100.1   56   28   69   27   104   31.9   59.6   68   49.6   78   70   89.4   915   105   101   90   13.0   7   60

The Gift of Gab

Add.

D. $\begin{array}{r} 0.5 \\ + 0.5 \end{array}$		I. $\begin{array}{r} 0.1 \\ + 0.6 \end{array}$	
L. $\begin{array}{r} 0.3 \\ + 0.5 \end{array}$		H. $\begin{array}{r} 0.6 \\ + 0.9 \end{array}$	
T. $\begin{array}{r} 0.4 \\ + 0.2 \end{array}$		C. $\begin{array}{r} 45.3 \\ + 10.2 \end{array}$	
E. $\begin{array}{r} 82.3 \\ + 101.4 \end{array}$	S. $\begin{array}{r} 17.3 \\ + 22.8 \end{array}$	O. $\begin{array}{r} 54.3 \\ + 45.2 \end{array}$	

A.
14.6 + 25.6 =

N.
2.6 + 24.3 =

M.
118.1 + 67.6 =

Y.
12.3 + 54.1 =

G.
7.5 + 29.4 =

W.
33.3 + 32.2 =

Why did the crow's mom take away her cell phone?
To solve the riddle, write each letter from above on its matching
numbered line or lines below.

$\overline{40.1}$ $\overline{1.5}$ $\overline{183.7}$ $\overline{185.7}$ $\overline{40.2}$ $\overline{1.0}$ $\overline{183.7}$ $\overline{0.6}$ $\overline{99.5}$ $\overline{99.5}$ $\overline{185.7}$ $\overline{40.2}$ $\overline{26.9}$ $\overline{66.4}$

$\overline{0.8}$ $\overline{99.5}$ $\overline{26.9}$ $\overline{36.9}$ $\overline{1.0}$ $\overline{0.7}$ $\overline{40.1}$ $\overline{0.6}$ $\overline{40.2}$ $\overline{26.9}$ $\overline{55.5}$ $\overline{183.7}$ $\overline{55.5}$ $\overline{40.2}$ $\overline{65.5}$ $\overline{40.1}$!

In Training

Subtract.
Color if correct.

R	S	U	N	I
1.5 − 0.8 = 0.7	63.4 − 57.8 = 5.4	7.5 − 3.6 = 3.9	108.2 − 94.7 = 13.5	1.2 − 0.6 = 1.6
T 25.1 − 16.4 = 9.7	**N** 99.1 − 24.9 = 74.2	**I** 2.1 − 0.9 = 1.2	**L** 480.3 − 358.9 = 120.6	**N** 79.4 − 5.9 = 73.5
	C 1.2 − 0.5 = 0.6	**G** 826.1 − 745.9 = 80.2	**R** 512.4 − 460.8 = 151.6	**W** 3.5 − 1.6 = 1.9
		A 50.3 − 19.4 = 30.9	**T** 961.3 − 809.5 = 151.8	**B** 12.2 − 4.8 = 4.7
			U 322.6 − 64.8 = 258.7	**E** 254.0 − 121.9 = 132.1
				R 170.2 − 5.9 = 164.3

What should you drink plenty of before a marathon?
To solve the riddle, write each colored letter from above in order
from left to right and top to bottom on the lines below.

___ ___ ___ ___ ___ ___ ___ ___

Name _____   Date _____

In the Future

Solve. Cross out each matching answer.

A. 4.3 + 6.2	B. 0.1 + 2.8	C. 4.4 − 3.2	D. 22.6 − 8.6	E. 3.3 + 1.2	F. 15.9 − 2.2
G. 4.7 + 2.4	H. 8.2 − 6.1	I. 7.5 − 2.4	J. 4.9 + 5.1	K. 8.0 + 4.3	L. 11.5 − 1.3
M. 0.7 + 3.5		N. 5.7 + 1.1	O. 7.8 − 2.5	P. 10.9 + 4.0	Q. 2.6 − 2.2

R. 40.4   S. 3.5   T. 8.3
   + 1.3   + 1.2   + 0.5

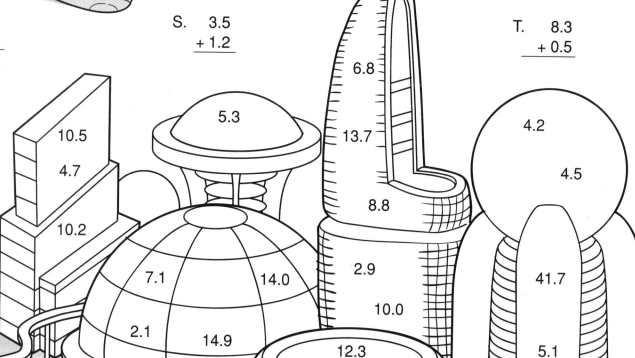

Math Practice Pages • ©The Mailbox® Books • TEC61122 • Key p. 95

Adding and subtracting tenths

Name

Date

On the Water

Add. Color the life preserver next to each even answer.

 A
15.16
+ 15.39

 B
35.99
+ 26.41

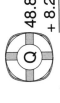 C
37.66
+ 4.08

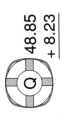 D
9.17
+ 7.33

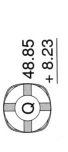 E
16.09
+ 4.06

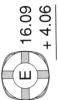 F
22.31
+ 1.02

 G
30.58
+ 15.22

 H
20.29
+ 4.18

I
85.95
+ 28.63

J
44.59
+ 5.33

K
71.72
+ 17.64

L
7.32
+ 5.08

 M
14.64
+ 11.34

N
55.84
+ 6.27

O
73.73
+ 9.54

P
30.62
+ 29.49

Q
48.85
+ 8.23

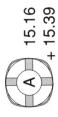 R
78.83
+ 65.96

S
84.73
+ 19.54

T
95.77
+ 42.89

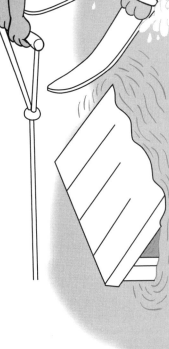

Music Downloads

Add.
Color the matching musical notes.

A. $21.61
   + $ 5.17

B. $12.95
   + $ 1.91

C. $41.58
   + $19.83

D. $ 7.32
   + $18.69

E. $253.76
   + $ 18.27

F. $ 3.12
   + $11.31

G. $178.54
   + $153.89

H. $5.07
   + $4.15

I. $446.18
   + $552.73

J. $14.45
   + $ 6.55

K. $9.33
   + $3.67

L. $503.25
   + $ 29.62

M. $45.91
   + $ 6.54

N. $10.48
   + $ 7.13

O. $312.85
   + $ 62.26

$14.86

$332.43

$61.41

$9.22

$14.43

$272.03

$532.87

$998.91

$17.61

$375.11

$13.00

$21.00

$52.45

$26.78

$26.01

Name _____   Date _____

The Royal Hat Shoppe

Subtract.

E. 7.04 − 3.99	K. 93.42 − 13.76	A. 87.52 − 35.47	R. 84.03 − 62.74
T. 34.23 − 3.49	A. 65.72 − 4.38	H. 74.88 − 9.99	S. 17.94 − 6.26
N. 24.63 − 13.48	H. 25.18 − 11.79		
C. 9.74 − 5.05	E. 32.47 − 28.55		
P. 21.36 − 18.47	I. 9.84 − 2.43		
G. 43.77 − 8.42	W. 64.22 − 27.61		

What kind of hat does Sir Lancelot wear?

To answer the riddle, write each letter from above on its matching numbered line or lines below.

_____ _____   _____ _____ _____ _____ _____   _____
64.89 3.92   36.61 3.05 52.05 21.29 11.68   61.34

" ___ ___ ___ ___ ___ ___ - ___ ___ ___ "!
   79.66 11.15 7.41 35.35 13.39 30.74   4.69 61.34 2.89

Math Practice Pages • ©The Mailbox® Books • TEC61122 • Key p. 96
Subtracting hundredths   79

Name _____   Date _____

Dancing Lessons

Subtract.

A. $7.11
   − $6.88

B. $26.31
   − $15.19

C. $4.12
   − $2.08

D. $80.60
   − $17.87

E. $304.67
   − $ 40.49

F. $73.84
   − $ 9.56

G. $121.41
   − $ 65.32

H. $412.34
   − $198.25

I. $273.23
   − $164.75

J. $5.92
   − $2.28

K. $74.92
   − $ 7.67

L. $69.73
   − $21.54

M. $42.30
   − $ 5.67

N. $57.30
   − $36.59

O. $3.76
   − $2.87

P. $468.32
   − $ 7.54

Q. $915.45
   − $ 67.09

R. $500.25
   − $ 0.67

S. $9.74
   − $5.05

T. $8.06
   − $3.19

U. $96.51
   − $61.23

V. $84.73
   − $12.45

Name _____   Date _____

Penalty Kick

Add. Write the letter of your answer in the box. Some letters will not be used.

☐ 6.35 + 4.2   ☐ 3 + 2.47   ☐ 4.66 + 2.7   ☐ 19.6 + 0.82   ☐ 8.42 + 0.8   ☐ 5.91 + 2.4

☐ 9.6 + 0.04   ☐ 34.51 + 9.5   ☐ 46.7 + 8.68   ☐ 7.3 + 7.19   ☐ 32.99 +10.6   ☐ 8.61 + 4.3

☐ 23.85 + 6.5   ☐ 11.73 + 4.1   ☐ 7.5 + 2.27   ☐ 41.72 +30   ☐ 10.95 + 4.8

☐ 1.47 + 0.5   ☐ 14.82 +12.2   ☐ 5.8 + 3.14

A. 14.49
B. 9.77
F. 8.31
C. 44.01
H. 55.38
K. 27.02
G. 30.35
I. 1.97
J. 15.75
E. 43.59
D. 9.64
N. 8.94
V. 5.47
L. 71.72
M. 12.91
U. 20.42
P. 15.83
Q. 9.22
S. 3.84
T. 10.55
O. 0.37
R. 7.36

Name _____   Date _____

Down by the River

Subtract.

A. 12.48 − 1.3	B. 9.75 − 6.4	C. 28.25 − 5.5	D. 40.7 − 20.53

E. 36.6 − 25.11	F. 742.9 − 31.75	G. 36.8 − 0.75

H. 16.42 − 6.2	I. 8.47 − 8.1	J. 5.8 − 4.61	K. 7.54 − 2.1

L. 18.8 − 4.51	M. 14.5 − 3.07	N. 180.63 − 10.4	O. 12.5 − 10.75

P. 8.43 − 6.8	Q. 224.7 −124.62	R. 65.84 − 4.6

S. 24.5 − 3.23	T. 15.8 − 7.62

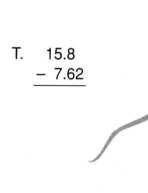

Subtracting tenths and hundredths

Name _____ Date _____

Paper or Plastic? ───────────

Solve.

1. Food and More sells large bags of apples. One bag weighs 5.73 pounds. The second bag weighs 6.45 pounds. How much do the two bags weigh altogether?

2. A bag of chips weighs 9.2 ounces. A candy bar weighs 8.8 ounces. How much do the two items weigh altogether?

3. One box of crackers has 98.2 calories per serving. Another box of crackers has 6.3 more calories per serving. How many calories are in one serving of the second box of crackers?

4. One bag of red grapes weighs 28.2 ounces. One bag of white grapes weighs 4.3 ounces more. How much does a bag of white grapes weigh?

5. On Friday, Food and More sold 21.85 pounds of chicken. On Saturday, the store sold 17.49 pounds. How many pounds of chicken were sold in all?

6. In aisle four, 15.4 liters of soda were spilled. In aisle ten, 3.2 liters of milk were spilled. How many liters of liquid were spilled in total?

Name _____   Date _____

Hooked! ━━━━━━━━━━━━━━━━━━━━

Solve.

1. Sara catches a bass that weighs 1.89 pounds. She catches a catfish that weighs 1.6 pounds. How many more pounds does the bass weigh than the catfish?

2. Billy gives Sara a sandwich that weighs 3.4 ounces. She eats 2.86 ounces of it. How many ounces of the sandwich are left?

3. Billy buys 19.3 ounces of bait at the store. He spills 6.54 ounces. How many ounces of bait does he have left?

4. Sara brings a cooler that holds 10 gallons of water. She and Billy drink 1.2 gallons. How much water is left in the cooler?

5. It takes Sara 1.7 hours to catch her first fish. It takes Billy 1.23 hours. How much longer does it take Sara to catch a fish than Billy?

6. Sara and Billy fish for a total of 8.79 hours. They swim for another 3.2 hours. How many more hours do they fish than swim?

Name _____ Date _____

Counting Sheep

Round to the nearest whole number to estimate each sum.

B. 24.3 + 2.6 =

L. 19.55 + 7.56 =

E. 30.47 + 4.06 =

P. 17.17 + 7.31 =

I. 9.82 + 1.4 =

Y. 74.6 + 3.84 =

S. 5.75 + 3.4 =

G. 39.1 + 4.67 =

N. 13.5 + 4.72 =

A. 36.9
  + 5.09

T. 6.38
  + 4.2

E. 540.5
  + 62.59

H. 100.5
  + 25.07

N. 49.17
  + 8.7

G. 53.42
  + 5.5

How do you not sleep for six days but still get plenty of sleep?
To solve the riddle, write each letter from above on its
matching numbered line below.

— —   — — — — — — — —   — —   — — — — —
27 79   9 28 34 604 24 11 19 59   42 10   58 11 44 126 10

Catch and Release

Round to the nearest whole number to estimate each difference. Cross out each matching answer.

A. 50.5
  − 12.3

B. 56.2
  − 17.5

C. 24.7
  − 8.2

D. 145.2
  − 83.7

E. 25.1
  − 16.4

F. 65.72
  − 8.59

G. 34.78
  − 12.93

H. 505.6
  − 82.8

I. 75.43
  − 4.88

J. 88.4
  − 7.82

K. 48.79
  − 23.1

L. 5.68 − 3.2 =

M. 4.9 − 2.07 =

N. 10.3 − 2.57 =

O. 9.82 − 5.5 =

Answer Keys

Page 4
A. 451,423
B. 5,782,941
C. 428
D. 4,586
E. 54,639
F. 84,235
G. five thousand, six hundred forty-nine
H. six million, seven hundred ninety-one thousand, two hundred fifty-six
I. eight hundred forty-three thousand, two hundred fourteen
J. seven thousand, eight hundred seventy-nine

Page 5
TO GET A FILLING

E. 34,5⑧9   A. 679,④86   F. 3,40②,257
T. ③,456,780   G. 49,37⑤   O. 901,2①3
I. ⑥04,634   L. ⑨,823,659   N. 8⑦2,312

"OAK-MEAL"

O. 2①,323   L. 405,3③4
A. 5,12④   E. 2②5,346
M. 33,⑦55   A. ⑤,234,365
         K. 5,⑥64,345

Page 6
A. 60   B. 3,300,000   C. 900   D. 4,000,000   E. 40
F. 100   G. 57,000   H. 7,000   I. 250,000   J. 100,000
K. 34,000   L. 220   M. 10   N. 2,500   O. 600

Page 7
A. >   B. <   C. >
D. <   E. <   F. =
G. >   H. >   I. <
J. >   K. >   L. =
M. <   N. >   O. =

Page 8
          A. 163   B. 141   C. 122   D. 141
E. 152   F. 156   G. 112   H. 160   I. 153
          J. 115   K. 131   L. 123   M. 121
N. 161   O. 180   P. 171   Q. 123
R. 130   S. 112   T. 146
U. 150   V. 144   W. 132
X. 140

Page 9
A. 507   B. 663   C. 3,700
D. 5,252   E. 841   F. 5,690
G. 321   H. 766   I. 8,237   J. 824   K. 5,707
                              L. 622   M. 730
                              N. 2,659   O. 413

Page 10
A. 76   B. 27   C. 19   D. 38
E. 35   F. 17   G. 18   H. 7
I. 6   J. 37   K. 15   L. 26
M. 68   N. 28   O. 8   P. 59
Q. 58   R. 36

Page 11

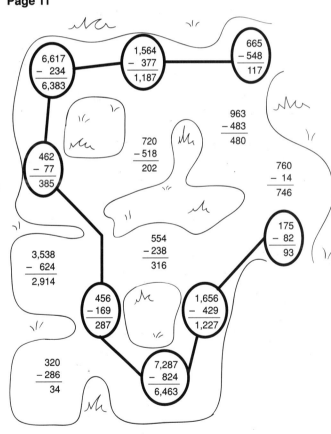

Page 12

A. 27	B. 87	C. 5		K. 8,299
D. 182	E. 116	F. 554	L. 9,853	M. 78
G. 8,604	H. 383		N. 400	O. 125
I. 45		P. 4,536	Q. 5,255	R. 4,367
J. 582			S. 231	T. 168

Page 13

(A.) 407 − 253 = 154	(H.) 4,700 − 186 = 4,514	(E.) 900 − 618 = 282	G. 3,903 − 692 = 3,211	(A.) 8,500 − 816 = 7,684
	(D.) 700 − 694 = 6	(R.) 4,070 − 794 = 3,276	I. 704 − 325 = 379	(A.) 5,041 − 785 = 4,256
(N.) 2,007 − 575 = 1,432	H. 600 − 475 = 125	M. 7,106 − 625 = 6,481	J. 760 − 531 = 229	
F. 3,000 − 983 = 2,017	L. 530 − 273 = 257	(D.) 6,010 − 478 = 5,532		
K. 170 − 121 = 49	C. 1,906 − 237 = 1,669			

A HEADBAND!

Page 14

A. 231 double-dip ice cream cones
B. 416 ice cream sandwiches
C. 367 shakes
D. 5,211 people
E. 457 fewer people
F. 9,916 ice cream cones
G. 178 more sundaes
H. 313 more gallons

Page 15

A. 140	B. 600	C. 400		
D. 0	E. 70	F. 700		
G. 200	H. 10	I. 300	J. 1,100	K. 0
			L. 1,600	M. 110
			N. 0	O. 1,300

Page 16

Page 17

A. 49	B. 72	C. 56	D. 27	E. 64	F. 14
G. 42	H. 80	I. 40	J. 24	K. 21	L. 81
M. 77	N. 36	O. 55	P. 54	Q. 48	R. 90
S. 63	T. 60				

Page 18

A. 90	B. 1,200	C. 1,500	D. 120
E. 810	F. 1,400	G. 400	H. 280
I. 1,200	J. 600		K. 640
L. 1,500			M. 560
N. 800			O. 540

Page 19

A. 1,500	B. 3,600	C. 3,500
D. 800	E. 6,300	F. 4,000
G. 3,200	H. 2,800	I. 3,000
J. 1,800	K. 900	L. 500
M. 6,000	N. 2,700	O. 4,000

Page 20
1. About 500 minutes
2. About 60 posters
3. About 2,100 seconds
4. About $2,000
5. About 800 cookies
6. About 400 bags

Page 24
1. 294 backup singers
2. 946 people
3. 372 minutes
4. 385 concerts
5. 880 autographs
6. 299 T-shirts

Page 21
A. 713   B. 169   C. 187   D. 840   E. 294   F. 407
G. 168   H. 492   I. 429   J. 672   K. 880   L. 714
M. 319   N. 308   O. 583

Page 25
A. 238   B. 192
C. 465   D. 960
E. 816   F. 468   G. 204
H. 216   I. 240   J. 221   K. 364
L. 564   M. 444   N. 224   O. 325

Page 22

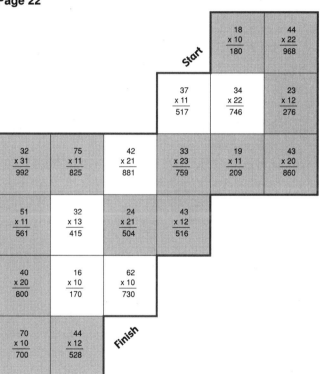

Page 26

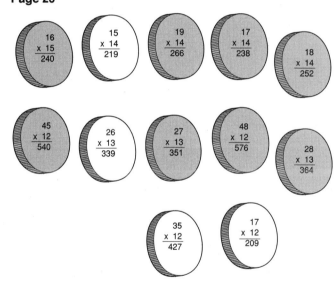

Page 27
G. 540   M. 312   A. 588   R. 255   Y. 481
L. 208   T. 228   U. 210   R. 224
A. 225   S. 819   R. 221
B. 444   G. 240   E. 552

BURGER ALARMS

Page 23
A. 529   B. 680   C. 403   E. 924
F. 288   K. 170   O. 957   Q. 726
R. 143   S. 861   U. 209
X. 308

A BOX OF QUACKERS!

Page 28
1. 240 cars
2. 98 tires
3. 276 minutes
4. 2,080 hours
5. 350 cars
6. 208 minutes

Page 29
A. 1,551
B. 2,808
C. 2,709
D. 5,358
E. 1,247
F. 7,050
G. 2,325
H. 1,392
I. 2,856
J. 2,695
K. 5,808
L. 1,755
M. 2,052
N. 462
O. 2,475
P. 3,185
Q. 1,496
R. 901
S. 6,408

Page 30
A. 2,075 B. 1,431 C. 2,584 D. 4,704 E. 1,755
F. 1,615 H. 6,298 I. 2,016 O. 2,898 R. 1,972 S. 4,950
          T. 2,478 U. 1,752 V. 871   Y. 3,096

BECAUSE THEY FIRE EVERYBODY!

Page 31

	A. 2,574	B. 2,408	C. 2,772	D. 1,170
E. 1,392	F. 8,188	G. 1,235	H. 5,546
I. 2,050	J. 1,885	K. 3,432
L. 414	M. 1,504	N. 7,200	O. 1,628	P. 4,158
Q. 8,740	R. 2,530	S. 1,518	T. 4,914

Page 32
1. 988 posters
2. 800 video games
3. 864 sunglasses
4. 1,680 lamps
5. 375 pieces of jewelry
6. 936 toys

Page 33

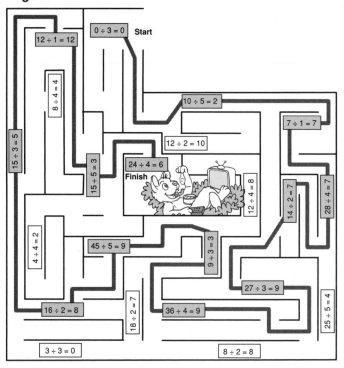

Page 34

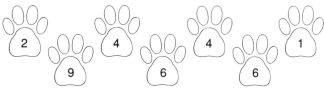

M. 7   O. 0   N. 1   R. 6   S. 4
T. 2   I. 3
U. 10   A. 5
C. 11   E. 9
B. 12   T. 8

BECAUSE IT TURNS ICE INTO MICE!

Page 35
A. 7   B. 8   C. 5
   70   80   50
   700   800   500
   7,000   8,000   5,000

D. 90   E. 90   F. 5,000   G. 500
H. 70   I. 6,000
J. 80   K. 20
L. 70
M. 400
N. 9,000
O. 90

Page 36

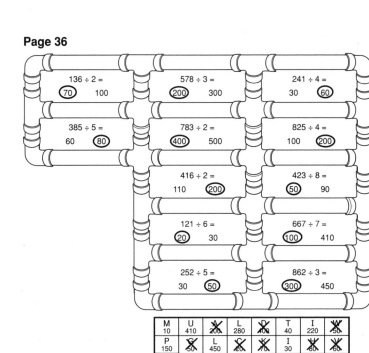

136 ÷ 2 = (70) 100
578 ÷ 3 = (200) 300
241 ÷ 4 = 30 (60)
385 ÷ 5 = 60 (80)
783 ÷ 2 = (400) 500
825 ÷ 4 = 100 (200)
416 ÷ 2 = 110 (200)
423 ÷ 8 = (50) 90
121 ÷ 6 = (20) 30
667 ÷ 7 = (100) 410
252 ÷ 5 = 30 (50)
862 ÷ 3 = (300) 450

M 10	U 410	X 200	L 280	X 400	T 40	I 220	X 50
P 150	X 50	L 450	X 20	X	I 30	X 80	X
X 800	X 200	E 90	X 100	R 340	X 200	S 130

MULTIPLIERS

Page 37

A. 80
B. 160
C. 70
D. 40
E. 60
F. 30
G. 60
H. 30
I. 80
J. 50
K. 90
L. 100
M. 90
N. 60
O. 70

Page 38

A. 26   B. 2   C. 9   D. 8   E. 6
F. 9   G. 4   H. 11   I. 7   J. 13
K. 5   L. 37   M. 6   N. 32   O. 17

Page 39

A. 12 R3   B. 13 R2   C. 18 R2
D. 19 R1   E. 14 R5   F. 13 R3   G. 13 R6
H. 12 R1   I. 21 R1   J. 12 R2   K. 21 R2   L. 15 R1
M. 11 R7   N. 16 R2   O. 15 R3

Page 40

A. 8 R2   B. 6 R2   C. 4 R5   D. 6 R4   E. 4 R2   F. 3 R3
G. 8 R3   H. 5 R3   I. 7 R4
J. 9 R1   K. 7 R1   L. 6 R1
M. 7 R2   N. 2 R3   O. 3 R2

Page 41

1. 9 fish
2. 6 groups with 4 left over or 7 groups
3. 8 times
4. 2 fish
5. 3 groups with 3 left over or 4 groups
6. 14 groups with 2 left over or 15 groups

Page 42

1. 5 kits
2. 9 boxes
3. 6 boxes
4. 2 parts
5. 3 trips
6. 7 T-shirts

Page 43

A. 124 R1   B. 123 R2   C. 214 R2   D. 127 R3   E. 138 R1   F. 137 R2
G. 368
H. 111
I. 261
J. 121   K. 164 R3   L. 223 R1   M. 113 R3   N. 299   O. 112

Page 44

A. 93	B. 63	C. 85 R1
D. 73 R1	E. 89 R1	F. 46 R2
G. 68	H. 87 R4	I. 27 R7
J. 51	K. 57	L. 66
M. 73	N. 36 R4	O. 93 R1

Page 49

1. ⅗	2. ⅝	3. 1⅜
4. ²/₄ = ½	5. ³/₆ = ½	6. ⁴/₁₀ = ⅖
7. ²/₄ = ½	8. ²/₆ = ⅓	9. ⁶/₉ = ⅔
10. 1½	11. 2¼	12. ⅜

Page 45

74	79	52	54	81	69 R4
86 R5	63 R1	64 R1	93	48	36 R3
		51 R1	47 R3	78	98 R1
		51	94 R1	34 R1	76 R5

Page 50

D ⅓ =	W ²/₄ =	L ⅚ =	T ⅔ =	Y ⅗ =	K ¹⁰/₁₂ =
(⁶/₁₈) ²/₅	⁶/₈ (⁴/₈)	(²⁵/₃₀) ²⁰/₃₀	(⁸/₁₂) ⁶/₁₅	⁶/₁₅ (⁹/₁₅)	(⁵/₆) ¾

P ⅜ =	M ⁶/₇ =	H ⅝ =	A ²/₄ =	O ⁴/₆ =
¹⁵/₃₀ (¹²/₃₂)	(³⁶/₄₂) ²⁴/₂₇	¹⁰/₂₄ (²⁰/₃₂)	⁴/₆ (¹⁰/₂₀)	(¹⁶/₂₄) ⁸/₁₆

B ²/₅ =	E ½ =	U ¾ =
(¹⁴/₃₅) ¹⁰/₁₀	(¹⁹/₃₈) ¹⁸/₃₈	⁹/₁₆ (⁶/₈)

S ⅞ =
¹⁵/₁₆ (²¹/₂₄)

It runs all <u>DAY</u> but never <u>WALKS</u>.
It often <u>BABBLES</u> but never <u>TALKS</u>.
It has a <u>BED</u> but never <u>SLEEPS</u>.
It has a <u>MOUTH</u> but never <u>EATS</u>.

<u>a river</u>

Page 46

A. 207 R1	B. 130 R2	C. 108 R3	D. 209	E. 101 R4
F. 110 R3	G. 106	H. 102	I. 107 R1	
J. 130 R1	K. 110 R5	L. 205		
M. 130 R1	N. 101	O. 140 R1		

Page 51

A. ½	I. 1	Q. ½
B. 1	J. ½	R. 1
C. ½	K. 0	S. ½
D. 0	L. ½	T. 0
E. ½	M. 1	U. ½
F. 1	N. ½	V. 1
G. ½	O. 0	W. ½
H. 0	P. ½	X. 0

Page 47

A. 106 R2	M. 110 R1	H. 308 R1	R. 110 R3	I. 105 R2
N. 109	T. 101 R4	B. 103 R4	E. 109 R5	D. 103 R3
			C. 106	
			S. 109 R2	

<u>BECAUSE HE HAD A BRAINSTORM</u>

Page 48

1. 105 movies	2. 106 games
3. 137 boxes	4. 183 videos
5. 49 pounds	6. 34 movies

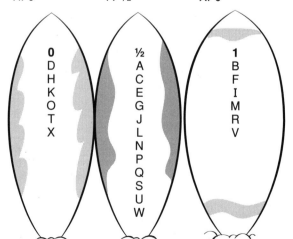

0
D
H
K
O
T
X

½
A
C
E
G
J
L
N
P
Q
S
U
W

1
B
F
I
M
R
V

Page 52

E. 2/9, 4/9, 7/9
A. 2/5, 3/5, 4/5
Y. 2/7, 3/7, 5/7
G. 1/8, 2/8, 7/8
R. 1/10, 3/10, 7/10
F. 3/16, 7/16, 11/16
M. 1/12, 5/12, 11/12
W. 1/15, 4/15, 14/15
I. 2/11, 5/11, 7/11
S. 1/3, 2/3, 3/3
P. 3/14, 7/14, 9/14
L. 8/20, 10/20, 18/20
M. 1/25, 10/25, 18/25
S. 1/4, 2/4, 3/4
O. 5/50, 15/50, 25/50

If <u>APRIL</u> showers bring <u>MAY</u> flowers, then what do May <u>FLOWERS</u> bring? <u>PILGRIMS</u>!

Page 53

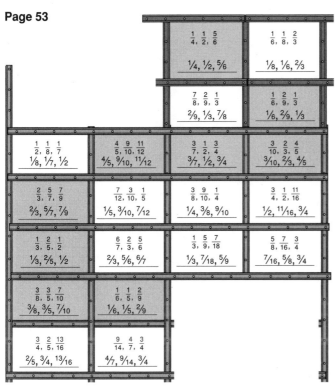

Page 54

A.

3	3, 6, 9, (12) 15, 18, 21, 24, 27
4	4, 8, (12) 16, 20, 24, 28, 32, 36

B.

2	2, 4, 6, 8, (10) 12, 14, 16, 18
5	5, (10) 15, 20, 25, 30, 35, 40, 45

C.

7	7, 14, 21, 28, 35, 42, 49, 56, (63)
9	9, 18, 27, 36, 45, 54, (63) 72, 81

D.

3	3, 6, 9, 12, 15, 18, 21, (24) 27
8	8, 16, (24) 32, 40, 48, 56, 64, 72

E.

2	2, (4) 6, 8, 10, 12, 14, 16, 18
4	(4) 8, 12, 16, 20, 24, 28, 32, 36

F.

3	3, 6, (9) 12, 15, 18, 21, 24, 27
9	(9) 18, 27, 36, 45, 54, 63, 72, 81

G.

4	4, 8, 12, 16, (20) 24, 28, 32, 36
5	5, 10, 15, (20) 25, 30, 35, 40, 45

H.

2	2, 4, (6) 8, 10, 12, 14, 16, 18
6	(6) 12, 18, 24, 30, 36, 42, 48, 54

I.

9	9, 18, 27, (36) 45, 54, 63, 72, 81
4	4, 8, 12, 16, 20, 24, 28, 32, (36)

J.

12	(12) 24, 36, 48, 60, 72, 84, 96, 108
3	3, 6, 9, (12) 15, 18, 21, 24, 27

K.

6	6, 12, 18, (24) 30, 36, 42, 48, 54
8	8, 16, (24) 32, 40, 48, 56, 64, 72

L.

2	2, 4, 6, 8, 10, 12, (14) 16, 18
7	7, (14) 21, 28, 35, 42, 49, 56, 63

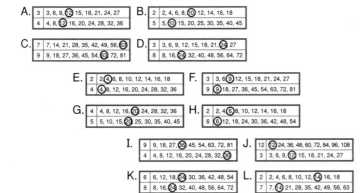

Page 55

1.	3 and 6	K 1	W 2	**L 3**	J 6
2.	4 and 8	**D 4**	O 2	C 1	I 8
3.	10 and 20	F 5	**A 10**	X 20	H 2
4.	16 and 32	U 4	**O 16**	R 8	G 2
5.	6 and 12	H 3	S 4	**R 6**	F 12
6.	4 and 14	A 1	E 4	V 7	**T 2**
7.	28 and 35	M 2	T 4	K 5	**S 7**
8.	18 and 27	N 3	**B 9**	W 1	E 27
9.	5 and 10	**E 5**	G 10	X 1	A 15
10.	2 and 28	D 1	S 7	**G 2**	M 6

11.	12 and 32	Q 2	**M 4**	E 3	A 8
12.	3 and 18	I 6	Y 2	**A 3**	B 9
13.	7 and 63	D 1	P 9	O 21	**N 7**
14.	25 and 65	**V 5**	T 25	D 1	J 13
15.	6 and 14	J 3	**I 2**	Z 7	Q 6
16.	8 and 28	P 2	L 7	**H 4**	C 8
17.	15 and 36	B 1	C 6	V 5	**E 3**
18.	4 and 32	L 2	U 1	**R 4**	I 16
19.	20 and 80	**P 20**	F 2	Y 4	N 10
20.	17 and 34	B 1	**S 17**	R 2	Z 34

<u>LABRADOR</u> <u>RETRIEVERS</u>, <u>GERMAN</u> <u>SHEPHERDS</u>, and <u>BELGIAN</u> <u>MALINOIS</u>

Page 56

A. 1/2
B. 1/5
C. 1/4
D. 1/2
E. 5/6
F. 1/3
G. 1/2
H. 3/4
I. 3/4
J. 2/5
K. 2/3
L. 2/3
M. 2/5
N. 1/8
O. 1/6

Page 57

A. 7 5/7
B. 27/7
C. 18 1/2
D. 71/8
E. 2 4/5
F. 67/4
G. 2 2/3
H. 33/8
I. 5/2
J. 73/5
K. 7
L. 11/3
M. 83/8
N. 4 1/3
O. 5 4/5
P. 4 1/2
Q. 29/12
R. 1 7/8
S. 8
T. 34/5

Page 58

A. 3/4
B. 4/13
C. 5/7
D. 4/5
E. 7/9
F. 2/3
G. 3/5
H. 1
I. 6/7
J. 16/21
K. 8/11
L. 12/17

Page 59

A. 4/11
B. 1/3
C. 2/5
D. 4/17
E. 2/21
F. 1/5
G. 2/9
H. 4/7
I. 13/15
J. 12/19
K. 10/23
L. 3/7
M. 4/9
N. 7/11
O. 5/7
P. 2/15
Q. 5/13
R. 0
S. 1/4
T. 23/50

Page 60

A. $\frac{2}{5} + \frac{1}{5} = \frac{3}{5}$ B. $\frac{3}{5} - \frac{1}{5} = \frac{2}{5}$ C. $\frac{3}{4} - \frac{1}{4} = \frac{1}{2}$

D. $\frac{5}{9} + \frac{1}{9} = \frac{2}{3}$ E. $\frac{8}{15} - \frac{2}{15} = \frac{2}{5}$ F. $\frac{5}{12} + \frac{5}{12} = \frac{5}{6}$

G. $\frac{1}{3} + \frac{1}{3} = \frac{2}{3}$ H. $\frac{5}{6} - \frac{1}{6} = \frac{2}{3}$ I. $\frac{3}{8} + \frac{5}{8} = 1$

J. $\frac{8}{9} - \frac{2}{9} = \frac{2}{3}$ K. $\frac{3}{14} - \frac{1}{14} = \frac{1}{7}$ L. $\frac{3}{10} + \frac{7}{10} = 1$

M. $\frac{9}{14} - \frac{5}{14} = \frac{2}{7}$ N. $\frac{4}{11} + \frac{6}{11} = \frac{10}{11}$

O. $\frac{2}{3} - \frac{1}{3} = \frac{1}{3}$ P. $\frac{6}{15} + \frac{4}{15} = \frac{2}{3}$

Q. $\frac{2}{7} + \frac{4}{7} = \frac{6}{7}$ R. $\frac{5}{12} - \frac{1}{12} = \frac{1}{3}$

S. $\frac{4}{5} - \frac{2}{5} = \frac{2}{5}$ T. $\frac{1}{3} + \frac{2}{3} = 1$

Page 61

$\frac{1}{6} + \frac{5}{6} = \frac{2}{3}$	$\frac{4}{15} + \frac{9}{15} = \frac{3}{5}$	$\frac{3}{5} - \frac{1}{5} = \frac{2}{5}$
$\frac{5}{8} - \frac{1}{8} = \frac{6}{8}$	$\frac{4}{7} - \frac{2}{7} = \frac{1}{7}$	$\frac{1}{4} + \frac{3}{4} = 1$
$\frac{5}{14} + \frac{3}{14} = \frac{5}{7}$	$\frac{7}{20} + \frac{3}{20} = \frac{1}{2}$	$\frac{7}{8} - \frac{1}{8} = \frac{3}{4}$
$\frac{3}{5} - \frac{1}{5} = \frac{1}{5}$	$\frac{3}{8} + \frac{3}{8} = \frac{3}{4}$	$\frac{9}{10} - \frac{7}{10} = \frac{2}{5}$
$\frac{7}{12} - \frac{5}{12} = \frac{1}{6}$	$\frac{5}{6} - \frac{1}{6} = \frac{1}{2}$	$\frac{5}{16} + \frac{7}{16} = \frac{2}{3}$
$\frac{10}{21} - \frac{4}{21} = \frac{2}{7}$	$\frac{2}{9} + \frac{4}{9} = \frac{2}{3}$	$\frac{3}{5} + \frac{1}{5} = \frac{3}{4}$

Page 62
1. ¾ of the class
2. 7⁄7 or all of the class
3. ⅘ of the students
4. ½ of the class
5. ⅗ of the day
6. ⅔ or all of the class

Page 63
1. ½ of the pizza
2. 7⁄9 of the pizza
3. 9⁄10 of the pizza
4. ⅓ of the pizzas
5. ⅗ of the pizza
6. 7⁄12 of the sauce

Page 64
B. 6½ O. 9¾ N. 14 A. 10 6⁄7 D. 10 I. 11⅖ Y. 8⅓
R. 6⅓ C. 17 M. 12½ T. 11
K. 7⅕ W. 8 5⁄7 V. 16⅓ H. 5¼

<u>FORWARD I AM HEAVY; BACKWARD I AM NOT. WHAT AM I</u>?
<u>A TON</u>

Page 65

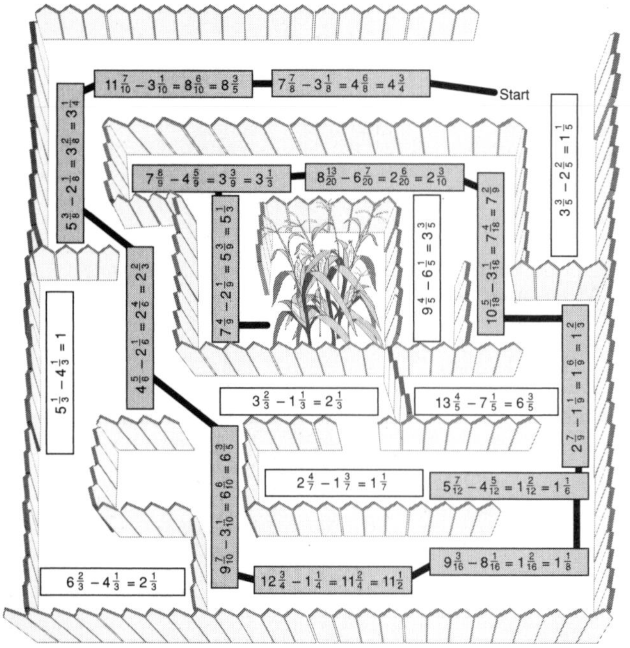

Page 66

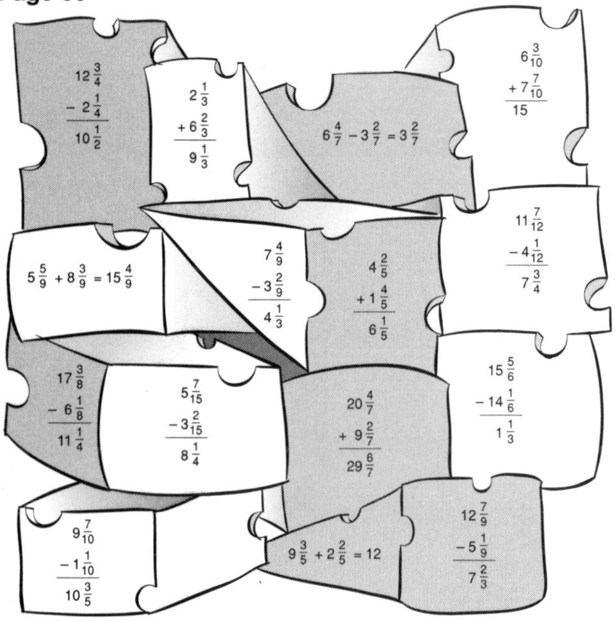

Page 67

$15\frac{1}{2}$	$7\frac{1}{2}$	$6\frac{6}{12}$	$7\frac{6}{12}$
$17\frac{1}{2}$	18	$18\frac{1}{2}$	17
$14\frac{3}{7}$	$13\frac{2}{7}$	$14\frac{1}{2}$	$1\frac{3}{7}$
$5\frac{4}{7}$	$11\frac{4}{7}$	$8\frac{8}{14}$	$8\frac{1}{2}$
$6\frac{1}{9}$	$7\frac{1}{9}$	$15\frac{1}{9}$	$3\frac{3}{9}$
$1\frac{1}{5}$	$1\frac{3}{5}$	$3\frac{3}{5}$	$3\frac{1}{5}$
$2\frac{4}{20}$	$2\frac{6}{20}$	$2\frac{1}{5}$	$2\frac{1}{2}$
17	$16\frac{1}{2}$	$16\frac{4}{5}$	$15\frac{5}{6}$
$29\frac{1}{4}$	$5\frac{1}{4}$	$5\frac{2}{5}$	$5\frac{2}{8}$
$13\frac{8}{11}$	$5\frac{5}{11}$	$5\frac{4}{11}$	$5\frac{8}{11}$
$11\frac{4}{5}$	7	$10\frac{1}{3}$	$12\frac{1}{3}$
$2\frac{2}{4}$	$2\frac{1}{8}$	$2\frac{1}{2}$	$2\frac{2}{8}$
$11\frac{3}{4}$	12	$7\frac{1}{2}$	$8\frac{1}{4}$
$2\frac{3}{5}$	$3\frac{2}{5}$	$\frac{2}{5}$	$2\frac{2}{5}$
$4\frac{8}{12}$	$4\frac{1}{2}$	$4\frac{2}{3}$	$4\frac{5}{6}$

Page 68
1. 2¾ cups
2. 4 cups
3. 4 cups
4. 4 hours
5. 4⅞ pounds
6. 4⅓ bags

Page 69

1. 1⅓ cups
2. 1¼ teaspoons
3. 1½ hours
4. 4⅘ ounces
5. 1⅔ cups
6. 6⅖ gallons

Page 70

A. 0.3, three tenths
B. 0.10 or 0.1, ten hundredths or one tenth
C. 0.28, twenty-eight hundredths
D. 0.8, eight tenths
E. 0.34, thirty-four hundredths
F. 0.9, nine tenths
G. 0.5, five tenths
H. 0.71, seventy-one hundredths
I. 0.6, six tenths
J. 0.27, twenty-seven hundredths
K. 0.1, one tenth
L. 0.54, fifty-four hundredths

Page 71

$0.5 = \frac{5}{10}$	$0.29 = \frac{29}{100}$	$0.60 = \frac{6}{10}$	$1.4 = \frac{14}{100}$	$6.03 = 6\frac{3}{10}$
$1.07 = 1\frac{17}{100}$	$0.35 = \frac{35}{100}$	$0.03 = \frac{3}{100}$	$0.2 = \frac{2}{10}$	$0.04 = \frac{4}{10}$
$0.8 = \frac{8}{100}$	$0.5 = \frac{5}{100}$	$2.91 = 2\frac{91}{10}$	$0.6 = \frac{6}{10}$	$4.144 = 4\frac{4}{100}$
$0.9 = \frac{9}{100}$	$5.1 = 5\frac{1}{100}$	$0.81 = \frac{81}{100}$	$0.44 = \frac{44}{100}$	$7.77 = 7\frac{7}{10}$
$3.60 = \frac{36}{100}$	$0.9 = \frac{9}{10}$	$0.35 = \frac{35}{10}$	$8.21 = 8\frac{2}{10}$	$0.05 = \frac{5}{10}$
$0.75 = \frac{75}{100}$	$2.02 = 2\frac{2}{10}$	$0.44 = \frac{44}{10}$	$5.8 = 5\frac{8}{100}$	$8.02 = 8\frac{82}{100}$
$3.09 = 3\frac{9}{10}$	$0.08 = \frac{8}{10}$	$0.16 = \frac{16}{100}$	$1.2 = 1\frac{2}{10}$	$9.11 = 9\frac{11}{10}$
$0.2 = \frac{2}{100}$	$6.4 = 6\frac{4}{100}$	$7.10 = 7\frac{1}{10}$	$9.98 = 9\frac{8}{10}$	$4.05 = 4\frac{5}{100}$

Page 72

A. 0.08, 0.9, 8.0
B. 61.73, 64.82, 64.87, 64.99
C. 17.09 **17.09**, 17.90 **17.89**, 17.89 **17.90**
D. 7.68, 7.8, 8.06, 8.7
E. 5.40 **5.39**, 5.41 **5.40**, 5.39 **5.41**
F. 2.31, 6.5, 9.86
G. 0.82 **0.80**, 0.81 **0.81**, 0.80 **0.82**
H. 0.21 **0.21**, 0.27 **0.22**, 0.22 **0.27**
I. 13.94, 13.95, 14.94
J. 1.7 **1.0**, 1.3 **1.3**, 1.0 **1.7**
K. 5.2 **4.95**, 5.17 **5.17**, 4.95 **5.2**
L. 6.53 **6.30**, 6.5 **6.35**, 6.35 **6.5**, 6.30 **6.53**
M. 45.07, 45.57, 45.7
N. 2.01, 2.05, 2.07
O. 23.0 **23.0**, 57.8 **41.03**, 41.03 **57.8**
P. 18.99, 19.10, 19.19

Page 73

A. 8.5   B. 7   C. 13.0   D. 915
E. 100.1   F. 69   G. 49.6   H. 70
I. 89.4   J. 28   K. 60   L. 78
M. 104   N. 259
O. 31.9   P. 59.6

Page 74

D. 1.0   I. 0.7
L. 0.8   H. 1.5
T. 0.6   C. 55.5
E. 183.7   S. 40.1   O. 99.5
A. 40.2   N. 26.9   M. 185.7
Y. 66.4   G. 36.9   W. 65.5

SHE MADE TOO MANY LONG DISTANCE CAWS!

Page 75

R	S	U	N	I
1.5 − 0.8 = 0.7	63.4 − 57.8 = 5.4	7.5 − 3.6 = 3.9	108.2 − 94.7 = 13.5	1.2 − 0.6 = 1.6

T	N	I	L	N
25.1 − 16.4 = 9.7	99.1 − 24.9 = 74.2	2.1 − 0.9 = 1.2	480.3 − 359.7 = 120.6	79.4 − 5.9 = 73.5

	C	G	R	W
	1.2 − 0.5 = 0.6	826.1 − 745.9 = 80.2	512.4 − 460.8 = 151.6	3.5 − 1.6 = 1.9

		A	T	B
		50.3 − 19.4 = 30.9	961.3 − 809.5 = 151.8	12.2 − 4.8 = 4.7

			U	E
			322.6 − 64.8 = 258.7	254.0 − 121.9 = 132.1

				R
				170.2 − 5.9 = 164.3

RUNNING WATER

Page 76

A. 10.5   B. 2.9   C. 1.2   D. 14.0   E. 4.5   F. 13.7
G. 7.1   H. 2.1   I. 5.1   J. 10.0   K. 12.3   L. 10.2
M. 4.2   N. 6.8   O. 5.3   P. 14.9   Q. 0.4
R. 41.7   S. 4.7   T. 8.8

Page 77

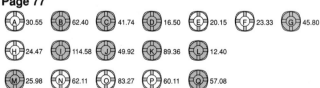

A. 30.55   B. 62.40   C. 41.74   D. 16.50   E. 20.15   F. 23.33   G. 45.80
H. 24.47   I. 114.58   J. 49.92   K. 89.36   L. 12.40
M. 25.98   N. 62.11   O. 83.27   P. 60.11   Q. 57.08
R. 144.79   S. 104.27   T. 138.66

Page 78

A. $26.78   B. $14.86   C. $61.41   D. $26.01   E. $272.03
F. $14.43   G. $332.43   H. $9.22   I. $998.91   J. $21.00
     K. $13.00   L. $532.87   M. $52.45
     N. $17.61   O. $375.11

Page 79

E. 3.05   K. 79.66   A. 52.05   R. 21.29
T. 30.74   A. 61.34   H. 64.89   S. 11.68
N. 11.15   H. 13.39
C. 4.69   E. 3.92
P. 2.89   I. 7.41
G. 35.35   W. 36.61

HE WEARS A "KNIGHT-CAP"!

Page 80

A. $0.23   B. $11.12   C. $2.04   D. $62.73   E. $264.18   F. $64.28
G. $56.09   H. $214.09   I. $108.48   J. $3.64   K. $67.25   L. $48.19
M. $36.63   N. $20.71   O. $0.89   P. $460.78
Q. $848.36   R. $499.58
S. $4.69   T. $4.87
U. $35.28   V. $72.28

Page 81

T 10.55	V 5.47	R 7.36	U 20.42	Q 9.22	F 8.31
D 9.64	C 44.01	H 55.38	A 14.49	E 43.59	M 12.91
G 30.35	P 15.83	B 9.77	L 71.72	J 15.75	
I 1.97	K 27.02	N 8.94			

Page 82

       A. 11.18   B. 3.35   C. 22.75   D. 20.17
   E. 11.49   F. 711.15   G. 36.05
H. 10.22   I. 0.37   J. 1.19   K. 5.44
L. 14.29   M. 11.43   N. 170.23   O. 1.75
P. 1.63   Q. 100.08   R. 61.24
S. 21.27   T. 8.18

Page 83

1. 12.18 pounds   2. 18.0 ounces
3. 104.5 calories   4. 32.5 ounces
5. 39.34 pounds
6. 18.6 liters

Page 84

1. 0.29 pounds   2. 0.54 ounces
3. 12.76 ounces   4. 8.8 gallons
5. 0.47 hours   6. 5.59 hours

Page 85

B. 27   L. 28   E. 34
P. 24   I. 11   Y. 79
S. 9   G. 44   N. 19
A. 42   T. 10
E. 604   H. 126
N. 58   G. 59

BY SLEEPING AT NIGHT

Page 86

A. 39   B. 38   C. 17   D. 61
E. 9   F. 57   G. 22   H. 423   I. 70
J. 80   K. 26   L. 3   M. 3
     N. 7   O. 4